LANGUAGE, FAITH AND SPACE:

THE DECLINE OF

FRANCOPHONE METHODISM IN

JERSEY 1900-1950

Rory Hill

Société Jersiaise

PUBLISHED BY

Société Jersiaise

7 Pier Road

St Helier

Jersey

JE2 4XW

Channel Islands

www.societe-jersiaise.org

First edition

Language, faith and space:

The decline of francophone Methodism in Jersey 1900-1950

by Rory Hill

Occasional Studies

Series number: 1

Text set in Ten Oldstyle

189x246mm

80 printed pages

Cover image: Sunday scholars from Philadelphie Chapel about to take part in a race during their Sunday school outing in July 1913. See page 51.

Contents

The Decalogue Board at St Martin's Methodist Church. Containing the Ten Commandments, the Lord's Prayer and Matthew 22 - The Greatest Commandment. The board was donated by Thomas W. Messervy in 1902.

David Marrett

Preface

This short book takes as its subject the Wesleyan Methodist Church in the island of Jersey from the start of the twentieth century to its mid-point. It focusses in particular on how the use of the French language within that Church declined and eventually disappeared, and it considers the social and spatial implications of such a change. The francophone Methodism of the Channel Islands was unique in many ways, receiving influences from the Huguenots and the Calvinism of the continent as well as the doctrine of John Wesley and the other Church fathers in Britain. Jersey, Guernsey, Alderney and Sark were among the first places where the Methodist faith was expressed in French but island Methodists were thereafter prominent in spreading it into France and other francophone territories.

Some readers may be surprised to learn that Methodism was not propagated in Jersey by a seed arrived directly from Britain, but rather one that came on a circuitous route from the cod fishing settlements of Newfoundland in the late eighteenth century. The Jersey soil in which that seed grew shaped the expression of the Methodist faith, most obviously, perhaps, in its language. The linguistic change from French to English that took place in the early twentieth century reflects wider social and cultural changes in the island during that period, and the reader may find a similar pattern in accounts of other religious, cultural and political institutions in Jersey and the other Channel Islands.

The archival work on which this book is based was carried out by the author between 2007 and 2009, drawing mostly upon collections in the Jersey Archive and the Lord Coutanche Library of the Société Jersiaise. Those archival materials were originally put to use as part of a historical geography dissertation completed at the University of Exeter in 2010, where a major research project was being undertaken into the historical geography of Methodism in Cornwall. Historical geography is a sub-discipline of geography concerned with processes in the past that have shaped the places we inhabit today. It is concerned with theoretical ideas as well as empirical research, and the topics of space, identity and power all figure prominently in recent work in that field. The present account is written from a theoretically-informed historical geographical angle, and it is hoped that the theoretical framing does not distract unduly from the coverage of the empirical material.

The Methodist Church in Jersey was and remains a welcoming home for its members. I am not a member, though I have ancestors who were. Accordingly, this account is not written by an 'insider', though it is written by somebody fascinated by the history of that Church and its members. The interpretive eye I cast over events in the past is done in a spirit of interested and critical academic enquiry, and is certainly not meant in a spirit of criticism. There are several detailed accounts of the history of Methodism and of particular Methodist chapels in Jersey listed in the bibliography to which the reader is encouraged to refer to gain a fuller impression of the subject treated in this short book. I hope that the present work, generously published by the Société Jersiaise, might encourage further investigation of the story of Methodism in Jersey, and of that eventful early twentieth century period of our island's history.

I express my thanks to Marie-Louise Backhurst, Roger Long, Glyn Burgess, Anna Baghiani, Gareth Syvret, John Le Gresley, Jean Treleven and Patrick Cahill for their invaluable assistance in bringing this book to print.

Rory Hill
February 2020

Introduction

One hundred years ago, there were no fewer than 30 Methodist chapels in regular use in the island, outnumbering the Anglican and Roman Catholic places of worship combined. Methodism had a profound influence on Jersey's society, and the expression of Methodism was itself shaped by Jersey's society. Nowhere is this clearer than in the language in which many Methodists articulated their faith. In the present study, local archival documents will be used within a social theoretical framework to examine how language was connected to faith, identity and politics in Jersey's French Wesleyan Methodist circuit between 1900 and 1950. The nature of the francophone Methodist community will be examined, together with the geographical pattern of its work, and the changes it underwent during that period.

The story of Methodism's origins in Jersey has been told through a number of island-wide and local chapel historical accounts.[1] It begins in 1774 with the heroic tale of two local fishermen, Jean Tentin and Jean Le Sueur, returning from Newfoundland impressed and moved by Methodist preaching. They began to build up a community in Jersey and following a request to John Wesley were sent a bilingual preacher. Wesley himself visited in 1787, his preaching, especially in the country parishes being translated sentence by sentence into French. Methodism went on to reach its apogee of island-wide popularity in the latter decades of the nineteenth century. In 1870, there were 2,435 members of the Wesleyan Methodist church, out of a total island population of circa 56,000, so that around 1 in 20 islanders was a Wesleyan Methodist member.[2] When members of the other Methodist churches in the island, relatives, friends and occasional visitors to chapel services are taken into account, it might be estimated that 1 in 10 islanders had an affiliation to a Methodist place of worship. And of the 2,435 members recorded in 1870, 1,839 were worshipping in French.

The French and Jersey-French languages have played a central role in Jersey life for hundreds of years. Like English, those languages have themselves developed and changed over time. Jersey-French (*Jèrriais*) is a form of Norman French, which spread to the Channel Islands from mainland Normandy after the settlement of the Vikings in that territory from the ninth century onward.[3] Though the islands remained loyal to King John of England after he lost mainland Normandy to King Philip II of France in 1204, English did not become the everyday language of the majority of the population of the Channel Islands until the nineteenth century. Before that, in Jersey, Jersey-French was the predominant language of conversation amongst local people and French the language of most formal interaction, such as court proceedings, church services and sittings of the States Assembly. Between the two languages there was, and is, a degree of intelligibility. It is supposed, for example, that when the French writer Victor Hugo lived in Jersey and then in Guernsey between 1851 and 1870, he did not speak English, yet he saw how it was gradually replacing the other languages.[4] In those same years, an education in English was being given to the young men of the islands in their respectively new and enlarged Victoria and Elizabeth Colleges.[5] This would presage a much wider adoption of English in education, commerce, and eventually government from the late Victorian period onward.[6]

Early in the nineteenth century, Wesleyan Methodism in Jersey had separated into an English and a French circuit. It is not easy to say when this happened exactly; indeed, it appears to have happened gradually over a number of years. 1808, 1818 and 1833 are all identified as significant dates of separation from a financial and record keeping point of view by the Channel Island Methodist historians Le Lièvre and Arnett, before the separation appeared on all official documents in 1838.[7] Previous to this, Methodist chapels held services in French and English at different times, and there is little reason to believe the split was acrimonious. Arnett, for instance, notes that the French circuit gave a donation of £550 to the English circuit for the construction of its own chapel in St Helier in 1827.[8] Both circuits served the island populace, though certain particular trends may be observed. The English circuit served the needs of the island's urban and suburban anglophone population, the English oyster fishermen in Gorey and of garrisons of British soldiers; the French circuit largely provided for the dispersed rural communities of the island, as well as for the French speaking population of St Helier in the form of Grove Place (later renamed Wesley Grove) Chapel. This latter chapel also had a symbolic importance for the French circuit given its large, central presence in the island's main town. Figure 1 shows the Methodist chapels in use between 1900 and 1950, including those on the Bible Christian (Great Union Road) and Primitive Methodist (Aquila Road) circuits.[9] From the turn of the twentieth century, membership numbers in both English and French Wesleyan circuits began to fall (in 1904 there were 1,400 total members of the Wesleyan Methodist circuits; in 1924, there were 1,266 members)[10] and, most relevant to this study, so did the established Methodist use of the French language.[11] By 1950, although membership numbers were not dramatically reduced, the French Wesleyan circuit itself was no more, both in the sense that the francophone expression of Methodism had been replaced in scheduled services, and in that the separate Wesleyan Methodist circuits in the island had re-united in 1947.

How did this happen? What was at stake in the decline of French and the re-organisation of Methodism in the island? Which voices clamoured in support and which called out in opposition? This is a chapter of the island's history, and an expression of the island's historical human geography, that has received very little critical academic attention. Yet it allows us to understand how the change in language, so often observed in historical work, if not interrogated in detail, was proposed, contested and gradually took place within one of the island's largest and most influential institutions.

Theoretical background

Scholars in cultural and historical geography have in recent years become interested in the spatial expression or what they sometimes call the *spatiality* of religious, political and other systems of thought. The presence, spread, size and style of places of worship, the parades and exhibitions of the faithful, the location and movement of religious communities, and the division of the world into symbolically sacred and profane spaces are all matters that have interested geographers, not to mention historians, anthropologists and other social scientists.[12]

Following the work of Lily Kong[13] in researching geographies of religion based within, and attentive to their specific social and cultural contexts, Catherine Brace, Adrian Bailey and David Harvey undertook a project that explored Cornish Methodism in the nineteenth century through a critical reading of historical church materials, popular accounts and personal testimonies.[14] Finding multiple interactions between religion and 'the construction and performance of everyday dynamic and hybrid place-based identities',[15] their ideas were developed analytically through studies of Methodist performance and ritual in space, and of the disciplining of young Methodist bodies within ecclesial discourses such as Temperance.[16] As part of the attention they paid to the fine-grained operations of identity and power through the theatre of religious expression, the authors argued that 'more research is needed on the 'language of Methodism' and its precise relationship with the 'rhythms of everyday life'.[17]

Substantial work in geography has indeed been carried out on the relationship of language to personal, group and national identity and the expression of power in different places. Drawing on earlier insights from scholars such as Janet Fishman, Eric Hobsbawm, Terence Ranger, and Benedict Anderson,[18] work has been completed on the symbiosis of vernacular expression and national identity in Britain's Celtic peripheries,[19] and on the various regions, including the Channel Islands, in which languages such as French have been implicated in symbolic and political struggles.[20] Yet the links *between* language and religion have not been thoroughly explored in human geography, despite significant empirical possibilities. In this study, and in the earlier dissertation on which it is based,[21] it is argued that it is in relation to matters of power, identity and community that the geographies of religion and language can most fruitfully be connected. Indeed, the rare studies that have examined such interaction offer accounts of religious and linguistic imperatives reflexively informing power relations and constructions of group identity; often in communities on the fringes of the British Isles.[22]

In examining questions of identity, power, belonging and distinction within a particular social context, it may be profitable to draw upon the theoretical ideas of French sociologist Pierre Bourdieu, particularly as they are expressed in his book *Language and Symbolic Power*.[23] Bourdieu argues for the place of language – both the choice of language and the use of particular words within a language – within webs of power relations that are built on different forms of capital and involve different sorts of performance. Capital, for Bourdieu, is not simply economic, but can also be social, cultural and symbolic, taking in the different domains in which people have skills, power, and recognition. Social capital may be the ability to draw upon influential friends; cultural capital the possession of a language, repertoire, or qualification; symbolic capital may be found in the wearing of a uniform, the carrying of a mace, or the uttering of distinctive phrases. Like economic capital, Bourdieu argues, people seek, defend and try to exchange other forms of capital, and these movements and contests may be seen as contours in the landscape of social activity.[24] The theoretical arguments of Bourdieu offer a potentially highly relevant means of interrogating the relationships between linguistic and religious practices in space, and it is at least interesting, and perhaps helpful, to consider this historical story of social and cultural change in Jersey through that theoretical lens.

This study will examine the nature and geographical expression of Jersey's French Wesleyan Methodist community in the period that saw its eventual decline. It will question the spatial patterns of worship and religious activity of its members, and assess the relationships of place, language and identity. The roles of bodily performance, notions of sacred space, linguistic perceptions, theological developments, changing social networks and discursive constructions of identity will be examined in exploring how processes of change in the island's society, or what after Bourdieu might be called its *social space*, related to changes in Methodist expression materialised in geographical space. In doing this, evidence from local archival materials will be read in the light of theoretical ideas from human geography as well as from Bourdieu and scholarship in the wider social sciences.

Mapping francophone Methodism

One hundred years ago, many of the services held at Ebenezer Methodist Chapel in Trinity, or Bethesda Chapel in St Peter, or Grove Place in St Helier, would have been in the French language. One hundred and twenty years ago, *most* of their services would have been held in French. Today though, all of their services are held in English. It appears that the decades of most rapid change from one language to another were those between 1910 and 1940. Evidence of this language change taking place in the French Wesleyan circuit is abundant in archival materials, and may also be ascertained from talking with those who lived during that period. The dissertation mentioned earlier drew upon interviews with several men and women who recalled experiences of Methodism in Jersey from their childhood and young adulthood.[25] The present study draws upon archival materials consulted between March 2007 and April 2009 in the Jersey Archive's Methodist Collection, and in smaller collections at the Lord Coutanche Library of the Société Jersiaise, the Public Library, and the Priaulx Library, Guernsey. Materials such as minute books and account ledgers generally contain a sudden change in the language of records from French to English. Where a note has been included to explain the change, this is rarely anything more than cursory; 'It was decided that in future the minutes be recorded in English' being a typical example. This begs the question of 'why?'[26] Perhaps in some cases, the secretary kept the minutes in French because he preferred it, or tradition dictated and the other members didn't challenge it. When a secretary retired, his replacement may not have felt as confident in French and so began keeping minutes in English: a phenomenon echoed in language changes in the drafting of legislation in the island over the same period.[27] But the fact of change remains. Circuit preaching plans, meanwhile, demonstrate a more progressive change through annotations to listed services often indicating the language to be used.[28]

In analysing and comparing these materials, it becomes clear that the decline in the use of French in Methodist services was neither simultaneous across chapels, nor disconnected from wider trends in Jersey society. Placing significant figures from these materials on maps helps us to view the situation across the island, to begin to analyse changes and then to explore potential causes. Figure 1 shows us that the numerous chapels of the French Wesleyan circuit are spread throughout the island and predominantly out of town. Figure 2 shows the relative sizes and constitutions of the island's French Wesleyan chapels in 1938,[29] and it may be noted therefrom that relatively small membership numbers are found in the rural south of the island, whilst further north, the rural chapels possess greater numbers. Figures 3 and 4, meanwhile, demonstrate the decline of French services throughout the island as shown in the materials in the Methodist Collection at the Jersey Archive. Figure 3 shows the year in which English minutes replaced French in the chapel Trustees' minute books (or similar materials where these were unavailable).[30] A general pattern emerges here in which chapels retain minutes in French for longer the further they are from St Helier, with northern parishes generally moving to English minutes later than the chapels of the south of the island. Figure 4 compares the number of English services held in 1910 with the number of French services in 1940.[31] The longer green bars show more English services being held in 1910, whilst the longer purple bars show more French language services still being held in 1940. Generally, this data shows that where more English services prevailed in 1910, fewer French services were retained by 1940. Here, again, it can be seen that with a few exceptions, the most rural, northern chapels of the island held more French services in 1940 than those in the south, where English services were already more popular in 1910, and where English Wesleyan circuit chapels were well attended. The general trend, therefore, is of a rural/urban division, where French Wesleyan expression is more prevalent in the country, with the areas closest to the town witnessing change more rapidly than those in more remote locations. In the following sections the processes that may have fashioned this geographical change will be examined.

LEGEND

- ■ Anglican (post-1800) Parish Church
- ■ Anglican (Original) Parish Church
- ▲ Roman Catholic Church
- ⬣ Baptist (Free) Church
- ⬣ Congregationalist (Free) Church
- ⬣ Salvation Army Hall
- ⬣ Free Evangelical Church
- ● Methodist (Bible Christ.) Chapel
- ● Methodist (Primitive Meth.) Chapel
- ● Methodist (English Wes.) Chapel
- ● Methodist (French Wes.) Chapel

op. 1900 - Year of opening (colour matched)
cl. 1950 - Year of opening (colour matched)
Gorey - Settlements

- Parish (Anglican & Civil) Boundary
- Major Road
- Railway
- Town Urban Area c.1934

N
E
0 0.5 1 1.5 2 2.5
1:54000
Kilometers

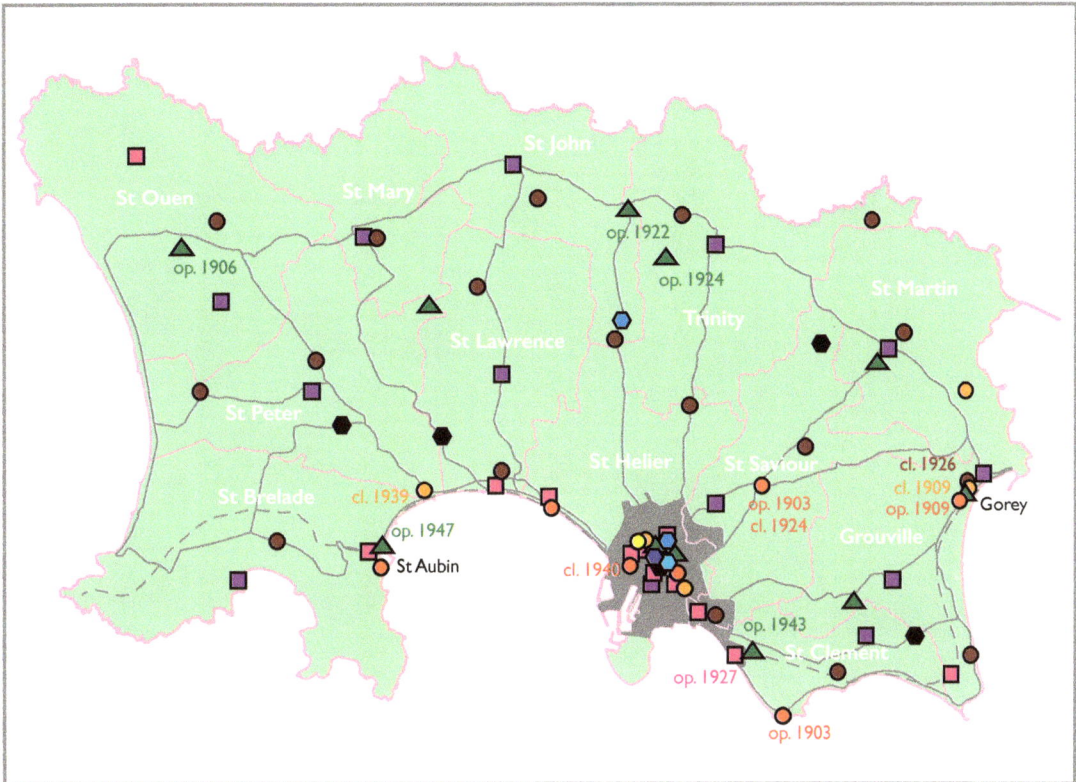

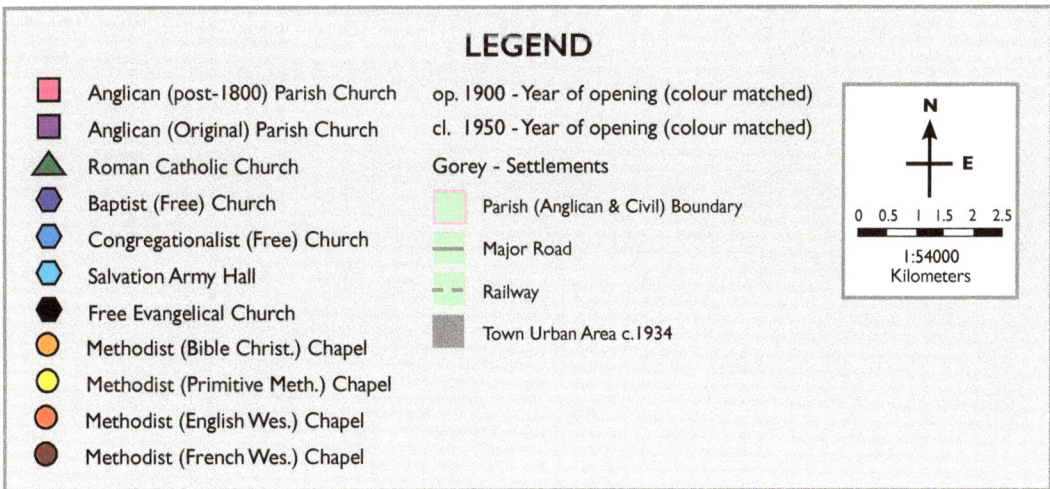

Figure 1: Distribution of religious in Jersey 1900-1950. Jersey and parish outline data provided by Digimap (Jersey), reproduced with permission of Government of Jersey   *Rory Hill*

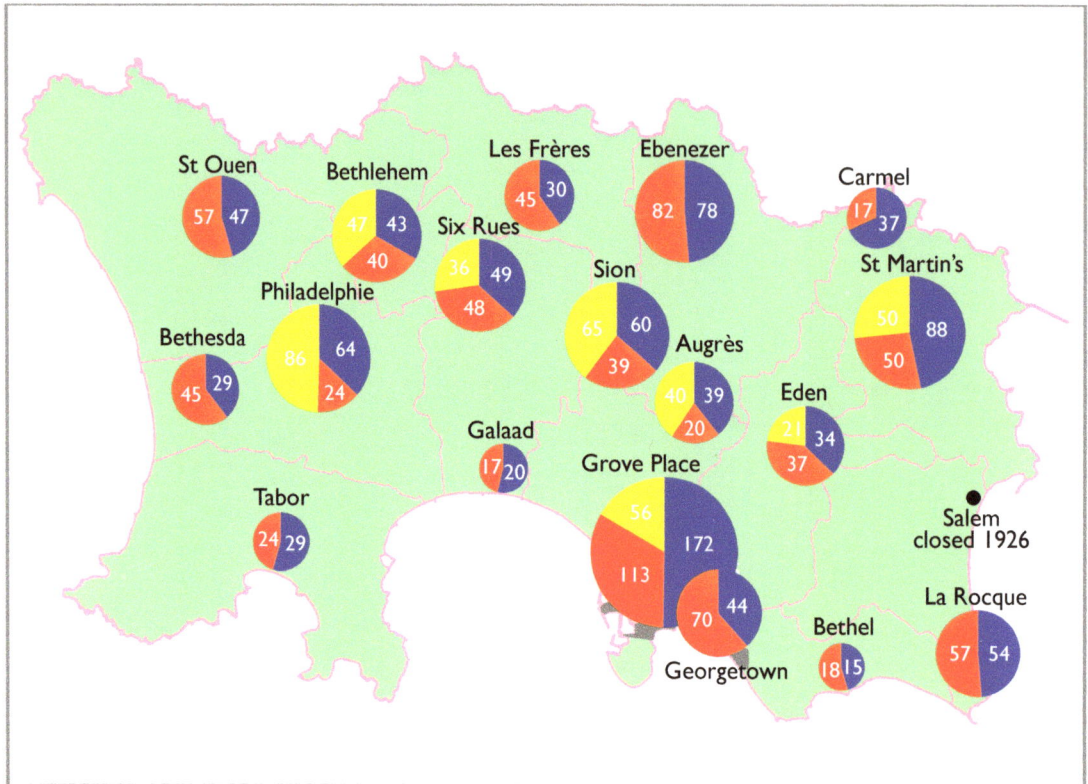

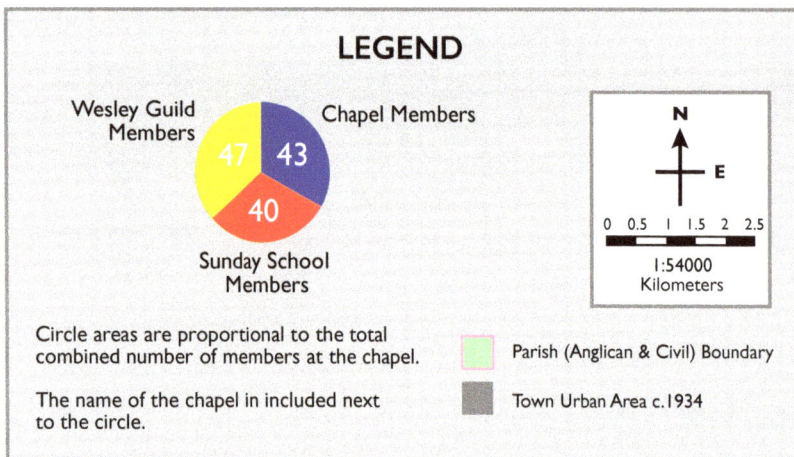

Figure 2: Relative size and constitution of French Wesleyan chapel membership (1938). Data in circles from Membership Schedule, 1938. Jersey and parish outline data provided by Digimap (Jersey), reproduced with permission of Government of Jersey   *Rory Hill*

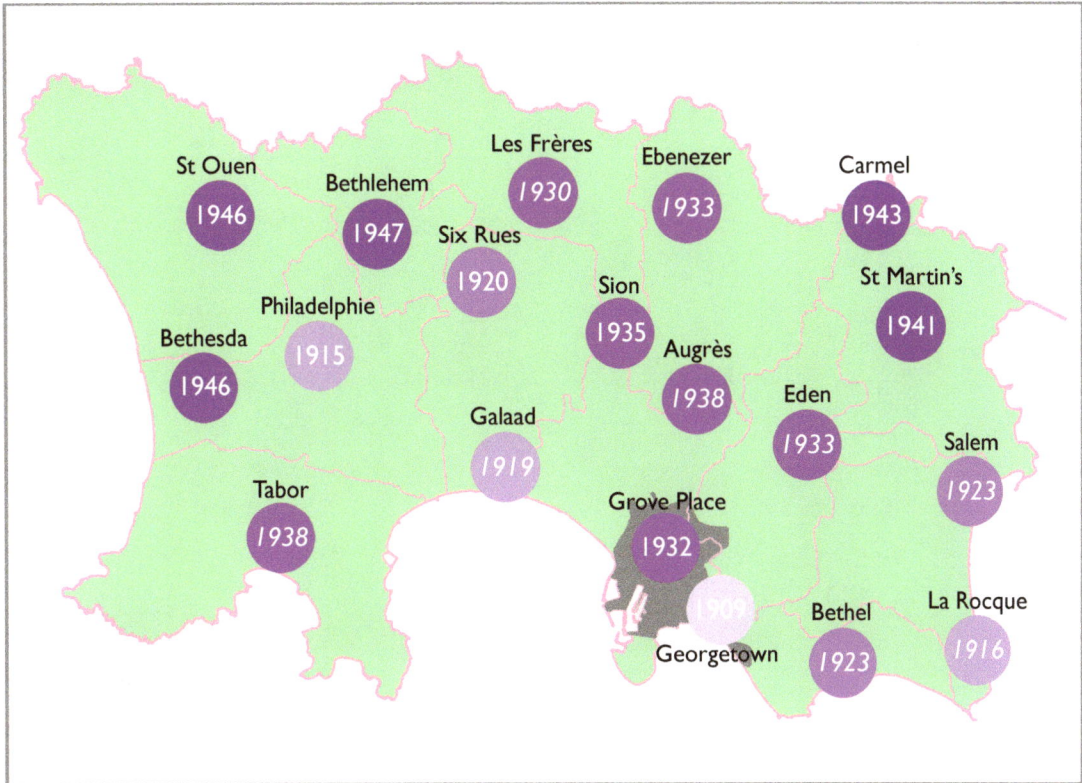

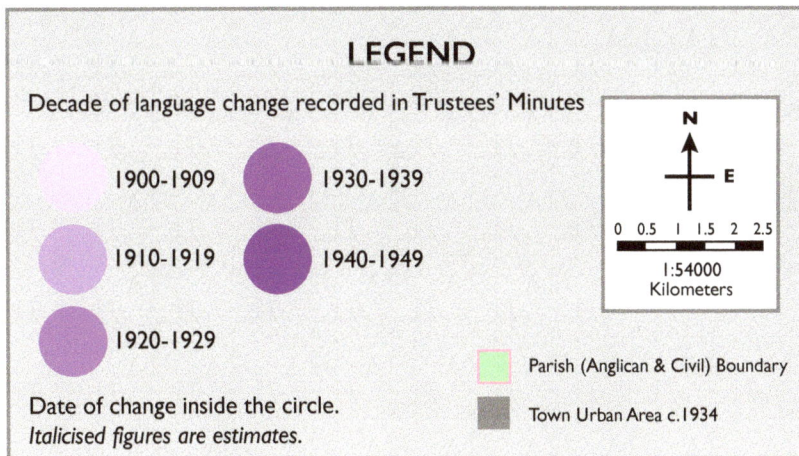

Figure 3: Years of change in French Wesleyan Chapel Trustees' Minute Books. Data in circles from Trustees' Minute Books and other materials. Jersey and parish outline data provided by Digimap (Jersey), reproduced with permission of Government of Jersey

Rory Hill

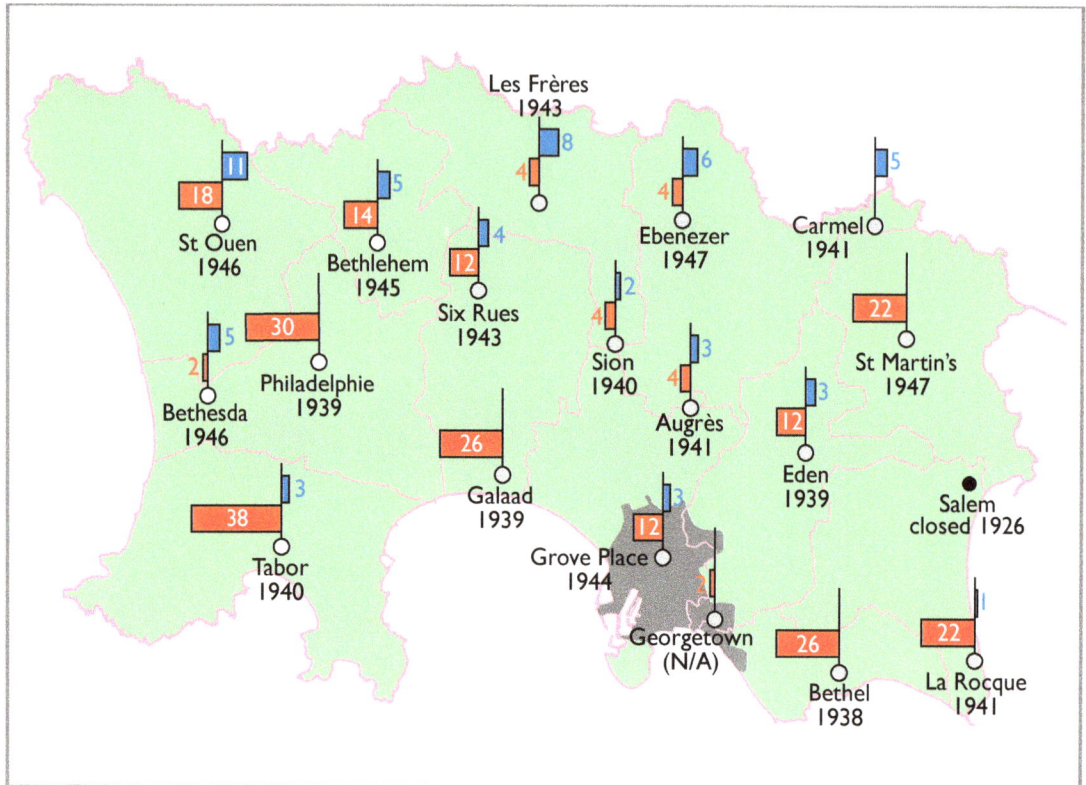

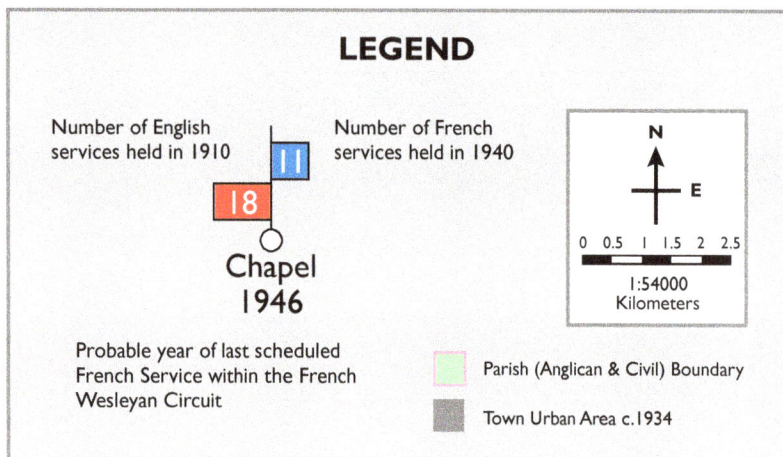

Figure 4: Comparative numbers of English and French Services in 1910 and 1940. Data in graphs from Circuit Plans. Jersey and parish outline data provided by Digimap (Jersey), reproduced with permission of Government of Jersey

Rory Hill

The Church inherited

Whilst the English Wesleyan circuit, and the anglophone Primitive Methodist and Bible Christian circuits, had chapels in St Helier and in the relatively built-up areas of St Aubin, Beaumont, First Tower, Samarès, Gorey and Five Oaks (as well as one at Les Landes in St Martin), Figure 1 shows that the French Wesleyan circuit dominated the rural areas of the island, particularly the northern parishes, and Figures 3 and 4 show that the use of the French language in chapels was a congruent spatial phenomenon. Such a geographical pattern has been identified by other writers assessing the distribution of the French and Jersey-French languages in the nineteenth and twentieth centuries.[32] John Kelleher argues in his *Triumph of the Country* that Jersey's rural population succeeded in protecting its particular way of life throughout the nineteenth century, and the rural identity peculiar to the island in the nineteenth and early twentieth century was readily conflated with, amongst other things, conservative stoicism of character, use of the Jersey-French (Jèrriais) language,[33] love of the island's farmed landscape, and attachment to one's local place of worship.[34] The performance of francophone language has been seen as constitutive of a particular sense of insular identity, with the ability, proclivity or determination to use the Jersey-French or French languages instead of English frequently connected to a sense of 'local islandness'.[35] In rural society, amongst farmers above all, Jersey-French was the established tongue, 'the language of the soil',[36] and of the networks of friends and family that lived on farms and in the clusters of houses and the few villages throughout the parishes.

The chapels of the French Wesleyan circuit were embedded in the social and spatial networks of their rural congregations, and many of the Trustees and members of chapels would have come from farming families. Hosting *'fêtes champêtres'*, summer bazaars and even plays with rural themes,[37] outside or in their school rooms, the chapels on the French Wesleyan circuit served as foci for celebrations of rural life and enactments of rural identity. A particularly popular and well-remembered rural activity was the Sunday school outing. Bailey *et al.*

and Harvey *et al.* have discussed, from their work on Cornwall, tea treats and parades as highly visible performances of Methodist identity and as organised consumption in and of particular spaces.[38] On Jersey's French Wesleyan circuit, records show that farmers from one chapel would transport the Sunday school scholars and leaders in horses and vans to another Chapel, the school room of which would host the tea, and a nearby field, common or bay would host games and activities. The accounts book of Bethel Chapel, for example, records visits from Bethesda Chapel in 1907 and from Les Frères and Bethlehem in 1914.[39] Georgetown Chapel records outings to Tabor in 1922 and to Bethlehem in 1924.[40] Both of these examples show relatively great distances being covered during the outing, but also show the journeys staying mostly within the rural parishes, within the social and spatial purview of the French circuit, as illustrated in Figures 12 and 13. The minutes of the Sunday school committee of Bethlehem Chapel, meanwhile, record the decision to precede a tea at Eden Chapel in August 1915 with a relaxing 'promenade' in the picturesque nearby valley of Grands Vaux.[41] It could be argued that through being driven by farmers along the lanes of the country parishes, and then being welcomed in a fraternal manner by another Chapel and enjoying organised recreation in its environs, the scholars, leaders and other Chapel members were discovering, expressing their sense of belonging to, and even projecting a sense of symbolic ownership over, the rural landscape of the island. Following William Jenkins's argument for religious identity negotiation in the context of particular places,[42] and arguments of Brace *et al.* for notions of Methodist community being rehearsed through performance,[43] it could be said these outings allowed for the identities, the senses of belonging of young rural Methodists, to be negotiated within rural spaces that were coterminous with the influence of their circuit. For adults, too, open-air services held amidst fields or above beaches facilitated a symbolic and material emplacement of the people and practices of francophone Methodism in the rural spaces of the island.[44]

In her autobiographical *Jersey Childhood*,[45] Doris Carter (née Sarre) recalls the place of the French language within Les Frères Chapel in the early decades of the twentieth century, and recounts with fondness the numerous everyday activities and interactions that were conducted in Jersey-French in rural life.

Indeed, her experience provides an illustration of the functional bilingualism or trilingualism that persisted in Jersey into the twentieth century, with French as the language of formal, ecclesial, political and legal affairs; Jersey-French the language of hearth, home and farmyard in rural areas; and English as a relatively recently-instituted language of education and intercourse with businesses in town and overseas.[46] For rural children at the start of the twentieth century, many interactions would have been in Jersey-French, whilst it is possible that the majority of their parents' interactions were in Jersey-French (such as in conversing with friends, family members and fellow farmers) or French (such as at Parish Assemblies). Meanwhile, for young and old alike, the Methodist chapel served as an important centre for the use of French – perhaps with a little Jersey-French inflection[47] – and Spence has even argued that through being the orthodox mode of expression in their chapel spaces, French enjoyed a popular recognition amongst Jersey's Methodists as 'la langue de Dieu'.[48] Thus the French language represented a form of cultural capital with important symbolic, religious, dimensions.

The nature of Methodist religion expressed in the chapel was itself coloured by its linguistic and social context. A. D. Gilbert has argued that the members of an association such as a local Methodist church circuit 'inevitably exert a powerful influence' on its character,[49] and David Hempton has suggested that throughout its historical and geographical development, the 'Methodist message was subtly altered by the social spaces in which it was expressed'.[50] Within farming communities particularly, Ole Riis has written that churches tend to maintain certain traditional values within the context of existing interpersonal networks,[51] and in Jersey, the character of francophone Methodism may indeed have been inflected by the existing social conventions, concerns and practices of its members. The importance of local networks is, for example, evident in the prominent role of Local Preachers.[52] Kelleher, writing of Jersey's rural Methodist communities, argued that:

> The emphasis on preaching, and more importantly, lay preaching, meant that country congregations received their dose of spiritual refreshment from their own peers and domesticity was emphasised from the very outset.[53]

Such domesticity was facilitated by speaker and listener sharing the same language, and often a similar background and sense of cultural identity. This proximity in social space meant that the distances covered in geographical space by Local Preachers – whether from Tabor to Bethlehem, or from Philadelphie to Les Frères – were largely immaterial. What kept the chapels on the French circuit connected were the social and cultural resources they had in common; chief among them the French language as a shared medium of expression. Though it is recognised as constitutive of the character of Methodist worship universally,[54] oral performance, delivered by Local Preachers, was of central importance to the spiritual life of French Wesleyan Methodism in the Channel Islands.[55]

It has also been argued that scripture and texts such as the catechism and hymn books were valorised within Sunday worship and as extramural 'treasuries of personal devotion'.[56] Once again, during the period in question, many of these were in the French language. Studied at home, memorised at Sunday school, read aloud in divine service, and even abridged and shared within locally-produced 'Quotation Books' sold to raise chapel funds,[57] the printed French words of Jersey Methodism were performed as part of the religious enterprise and of one's personal relationship with God. Indeed, a lecture delivered at the Local Preacher's Meeting in 1900 by Mr. C. W. Binet on the subject of *'Comment conduire un culte public'* propounded the central importance of *'le chant, la prière et la lecture de la parole de Dieu'.*[58] The rehearsal of speech and the written word in the French language within the ecclesial space served to reinforce the shared understanding of the Methodist faith from a rural Jersey perspective, and to maintain the value of francophone Methodist cultural resources, or what Bourdieu would call *cultural capital*, inherited from the circuit's antecedent members. Dedication, discipline and long service in propagating the faith and supporting the island's Methodist community were recognised by the group, such as in the certificate presented to Daniel Bisson, secretary of the local preachers association of the French Wesleyan circuit, and signed by his confrères (Figure 5). At chapel anniversary services, and in the compilation of chapel histories, the faith and work of elders and of previous generations of Methodists, many of whom would have been relatives of current members of the same chapel, were celebrated and presented as examples to

Figure 5: Certificate of appreciation of long service presented to Daniel Bisson on 8 December 1910 by the Assemblée des Prédicateurs Locaux du Circuit Français de l'Église Méthodiste Wesleyenne de Jersey

J/C/BN/B/8 - Jersey Heritage

follow.[59] And in the continued transmission of that faith and work, the nature of Jersey's francophone Methodism inevitably experienced a degree of isolation from developments in Britain and elsewhere.

Indeed it could be argued that, built upon the value of inherited text and oratory, francophone Methodism in Jersey in the early years of the twentieth century promoted a straightforward, scriptural understanding of the Christian faith.[60] Compiled before, and at a spatial remove from British Methodism's 'mahogany age' of liberal, sacramental theology,[61] the inherited canon on which Jersey Methodists relied – the circuit's symbolic resources – expressed the theological imperatives of past generations. Encouraged by the conservatism of Jersey's rural society,[62] and perhaps even bearing some traces of the island's Calvinist heritage,[63] Jersey's francophone Methodism could be described in terms of a certain unequivocal simplicity of doctrine. Mourant, for example, in her history of Eden Chapel, recounts how one Local Preacher taught a group of Sunday scholars the Lord's Prayer, but instead of concluding with the European French formula of '*aux siècles des siècles*', he delivered the perhaps less elegant but more familiar, direct and zealous expression '*à jamais!*'[64] Broughton, meanwhile, argues that its insular expression retained an emphasis on 'a simple message of "justification by faith" and the absolute supremacy of the Bible',[65] at the expense of wider social concerns and the idea of 'applied religion'.[66] Though there was of course awareness of world events and, for instance, considerable interest in overseas missions, the social programmes and discourses in which Methodists played leading roles in the industrial cities of Britain were simply less applicable to the Channel Islands. Isolated from the developments of British Methodism through distance and language, Jersey-born Local Preachers, and to a lesser extent Ministers, had less access, at the turn of the twentieth century, to the library of educational materials their English counterparts could draw from,[67] and so rehearsing the prayers and doxological formulae of their own teachers, these men delivered sermons with a directness facilitated by personal familiarity and fashioned by a partly insular theological inheritance.

Hymnody in the circuit was also coloured by the direct, scriptural evangelism of Jersey's francophone Methodism. Scholars of Methodism affirm the centrality of hymns to the theological emphases, ethos and character of worship in

Britain,[68] with Charles Wesley's compositions supported by his brother John's instruction to 'sing lustily and with good courage'.[69] In Jersey's French circuit, however, the majority of those hymns assembled in the *Recueils de Cantiques* were either descended from Huguenot collections, or composed anew by Jean de Quetteville, one of Jersey's earliest Methodist leaders, in the eighteenth and early nineteenth centuries.[70] Described by one historian as being '*aux airs souvent très chantants (parfois ronflants)*',[71] these were hymns embedded in the linguistic and theological spaces of Channel Island Methodism, and it could be asserted that they served to promulgate the practical interpretation and evangelistic expression of Methodism through their continued use. By the end of the nineteenth century, however, they were failing to reflect developments in hymnody in anglophone Britain. In sum, following Brace *et al.* and Kong,[72] these local and particular expressions of faith reflected a religion based within, and inseparable from, the society and culture from which it drew its adherents.

Authority and transgression:
the Dewhurst affair

Taking the idea that Methodists understood worship to be 'an arena in which individuals may encounter the living and holy God through prayer, singing and preaching',[73] and having found that such oral performance was delivered in the French language, it may be understood that the French Wesleyan Chapel was the locus of a spoken, sung and prayed expression of faith, performed by members of the congregation and those authorised to speak on its behalf. The French language was the solemn, formal, ecclesial mode of expression sanctioned and apposite in the chapel space, and customarily used to transmit the doctrine inherited from the chapel's founding members. It was, therefore, a symbolic resource at the heart of their religious community. For the Trustees of each chapel, the protective obligations of stewardship extended from the built materiality of the sacred space to the symbolic, even sacred nature of what was said within it. The geographer Fraser MacDonald has discussed the nonconformist tradition of sanctioning of doctrine within the chapel space.[74] Speaking on behalf of the group, representing the group, and exerting a kind of illocutionary or verbal power over the group – that is, the body of the church – the speaker, whether it is a Minister or Lay Preacher, fulfils a symbolically critical function through the expression of the group's religious faith. If the presbyters feel that the person in the pulpit is preaching errant doctrine, MacDonald writes, they may take it upon themselves to remove him or her for the good of the congregation.[75] Protecting the group from heterodox discourse in this way amounts to an effective form of censorship placed in the chapel; 'excluding agents from...the places which allow one to speak with authority.'[76]

On the French Wesleyan circuit in Jersey, though chapel Trustees were not exactly the same as presbyters in Presbyterian and similar non-conformist traditions, not having the authority to remove a minister (as this authority lay with the Connexion), the ecclesial space for which they were responsible was the subject of their vigilant protection from both errancy in doctrine and errancy in language. In these circumstances, it was inevitable that conflict would arise when, in 1903, on the advice of a Commission despatched to the island in the previous year, the Wesleyan Methodist Conference announced its intention to end the circuit's customary privilege of inviting its own French-speaking Minister to superintendence, and instead, to follow standard procedure by appointing its own choice of monoglot English-speaking Minister to lead purely English services.[77] The plans were greeted with disdain in the French Wesleyan circuit, and opposition crystallised amongst the Trustees of Grove Place Chapel. A vote of protest against the measure was taken at the September 1903 quarterly meeting, and a report outlining the bases for resistance to the plans (essentially, that French ministrations were required for a francophone circuit – the appointment of an English minister being potentially 'disastrous') was sent as a memorial to the national Conference of July 1904.[78]

Conference, in its reply, sought to placate the circuit, and expressed that it was not its intention to 'interfere' with its work.[79] These sentiments did not extend to revising its plans to appoint a solely anglophone Minister, however; only to postponing them. In 1906, therefore, news reached Grove Place that Conference was despatching such a Minister to take up a post in their French Wesleyan circuit; the Reverend E. E. Dewhurst.[80] Outraged, the chapel's Trustees took the extraordinary action of banning English services therein unless explicitly sanctioned by them; 'ce dans le but de conserver l'usage de la langue française dans la chapelle'.[81] They voted, furthermore, to consult the island's two Crown Officers for their legal opinions on the matter, and vowed, in any case, to refuse the new Minister the use of the pulpit, 'jusqu'à ce qu'il puisse prêcher en français'.[82] Closing ranks around the symbolic centre of francophone Methodist expression, the Trustees would not allow English ministrations authorised from without to take place in the chapel that was entrusted to them. Not only had the specific cultural capital of their Methodist community to be defended, but their 'assumed' authority over the expression of such capital in the chapel space also had to be maintained.

Aware of the controversy surrounding his appointment, a welcome reunion was held for Dewhurst in the winter of 1906 by other circuit Ministers in which the pressing question of '*La Langue Anglaise ou la Langue Française*' was explicitly considered.[83] The Reverend James Wood, a bilingual Guernseyman, is recorded as delivering the first discourse:

> Dans le cours d'une allocution, très suivie par son auditoire, le Rév. Wood traite la question épineuse de la nomination au Circuit Wesleyen Français d'un Pasteur ne parlant que l'anglais. On ne peut pas ignorer, dit-il, que dans les Chapelles Wesleyennes du Circuit, il est beaucoup de jeunes gens désireux d'avoir de temps à autre un service en langue anglaise et qui le réclament avec insistence. Il faut essayer de les garder dans l'Eglise et on doit bien faire quelque chose pour eux. Après tout, ne sommes nous pas tous sujets britanniques, n'est-ce pas ici un sol anglais (applaudissements)?[84]

> Translation: In the course of a short speech, closely followed by his audience, the Rev. Wood considered the thorny question of the nomination of a Pastor, only able to speak English, to the French Wesleyan Circuit. One cannot ignore, he said, that in the Wesleyan Chapels of the Circuit there are lots of young people keen to have from time to time a service in the English language, and who demand it. We must try to keep them in the Church and we really must do something for them. After all, are we not all British subjects, is this not an English soil (applause)?

Calling forth a shared identity based on Britishness served here to cement support for English services. In the company of a colleague recently arrived from the national Conference, the Ministers would have been unlikely to wish to portray themselves as far removed from it. And the Reverend Wood went on to repeat his request for a Christian sense of self-sacrifice to overcome the ingrained disposition towards French religious expression; abnegation for the benefit of children, who were just beginning to become accustomed to English through their compulsory education.

The Reverend Dewhurst himself was then invited to speak, and he asserted his determination to not be silenced by those who sought to prevent his English sermons from being delivered; with the following being recorded:

Quand il a eu une entrevue avec le Surintendent du Circuit, ce dernier l'a informé que les Séquestres de la Chapelle Grove-Place avaient passé une résolution d'après laquelle aucun service anglais ne devait être tenu dans leur lieu de culte (cris de c'est honteux!).

S'animant, l'orateur [Dewhurst] dit qu'il ne prendra pas d'ordres de Séquestres quelconques; il ne les acceptera que de son Surintendant (applaudissements). . . Il tient à la main deux lettres. . . elles lui disent qu'il est à Jersey pour prêcher anglais dans ce Circuit. . . ce n'est pas tant lui-même qu'il représente ici, c'est bien la Conférence Wesleyenne Méthodiste Anglaise; il laissera la Conférence soutenir la lutte pour lui et il ne doute pas que dans un avenir rapproché, il aura le plaisir de prêcher du haut de la chaire de Grove Place (applaudissements).[85]

Translation: When he had an interview with the Superintendent of the Circuit, the latter informed him that the Trustees of the Grove Place Chapel had passed a resolution according to which no English service could be held in their place of worship (cries of 'it's shameful'!)

Enlivened, the speaker [Dewhurst] said that he will not take the orders of any Trustee; he won't accept any orders but those of his Superintendent (applause). . . He holds in his hands two letters...they tell him that he is in Jersey to preach English in this Circuit. . . it is not so much himself that he represents here, it's rather the English Wesleyan Methodist Conference; he will let the Conference support the fight for him [to remain] and he doesn't doubt that in a more reconciled future, he will have the pleasure of preaching from the pulpit in Grove Place (applause).

The power struggle between the Trustees of Grove Place Chapel, and the national Conference and its designated representative is thus laid bare, with language closely implicated in matters of Methodist identity and authorised performance. Exhibiting his possession of letters carrying all of the symbolic weight of Conference, Dewhurst explicitly positioned himself as representative of a wider group, and as authorised vector of Conference discourse and power. In so doing, he supplemented his own subjective position as one fallible Minister in a circuit with the objective position as delegate of a powerful body,[86] and argued in that way for the seizure of the 'haut de la chaire de Grove Place' –

the locus of symbolic, illocutionary power at the centre of the island's French Wesleyan circuit; the locus of the transmission of the word of God.[87]

Notwithstanding written *projets* and petitions from Local Preachers and various chapel members,[88] the requested opinion of the island's Attorney General,[89] and correspondence with the President of the Wesleyan Methodist Conference, the Grove Place Trustees felt compelled '*par leur serment et leur conscience*' to maintain their position of resistance.[90] With their self-declared authority restated over the chapel space, Dewhurst remained barred from within, and there is evidence from March 1907 of his preaching in the less restricted space of the adjacent school room.[91] 'Stormy quarterly meetings' took place,[92] with one held on the 30th of March 1907 having to be adjourned to a later date because an uninvited Local Preacher refused to leave.[93] Minutes record that this meeting finally took place soon after, on the 13th of April, with the unprecedented condition imposed that all those who sought to enter had to produce their membership card to the group, under the supervision of a Policeman stationed at the door of the chapel.[94] Extraordinary scenes unfolded as, after the meeting had begun, some of those who had been barred from entering made their way in: the Reverend Dewhurst '*est entré dans la chapelle et a declaré l'assemblée illégale...puis s'est retiré*', followed by the later appearance of a Local Preacher, who entered and presented a formal protest to the assembly, also declaring it illegal, on the grounds that '*on a forcément refusé l'entrée au Revd. E. E. Dewhurst, et à un grand nombre d'autres membres de cette assemblée*'.[95] Indeed, the illegality of this meeting had been asserted by the President of the Conference, and was discussed at a meeting of the Channel Island District Synod in Guernsey the next month. There, delegates were told of the 'seething discontent' that was in evidence in Jersey, and there it was resolved to send a new Superintendent Minister to bring together the opposed elements of the French Wesleyan circuit.[96]

Such extraordinary scenes appear as the visible manifestation of a highly symbolic struggle. The constitution of the group, the identity of its members, the assumed authority of chapel over circuit and Conference, and the balance in the value of two forms of linguistic capital were all being disputed in a Methodist community that was beginning to fracture internally. In resisting the

Rev. Dewhurst's ability to perform from the pulpit of the chapel, the Trustees were refusing to recognise, and thus contribute to, his authority in that space.[97] Despite being invested by Conference with the symbolic authority of ministry, and thus theoretically possessed of a 'legitimate...universally recognized identity'[98] in Methodist communities, the Trustees of Grove Place exercised their own authority by placing the symbolic boundary between the autonomy of their francophone Methodist expression and the transgression of an imposed English version within the built space of the chapel. When Conference sought to dissolve this boundary, by authorising English ministrations in the circuit, both the value of the capital of francophone Methodism, and the peculiar identity of its possessors, were under threat. It is thus possible to imagine the parallels between the defence of linguistic and religious forms of capital, and the defence of a sense of group identity. The powerful and performed conflations between religion, language, and Jersey identity discussed in this section, however, would become more difficult to maintain in the face of developing discourses of British Methodism.

Figure 6: Certificate presented to Doris Le Cornu by the Sunday School Council of Wesley Street Methodist Church (English Circuit) in respect of the value of the scholar's prize being given up on 2 May 1915 'to relieve the wants of the heroic Belgians' during the First World War

J/C/BN/A/1 - *Jersey Heritage*

Performing union and discord

In the previous two chapters, it has been argued that francophone Methodism was a form of cultural and symbolic capital shared by members of the congregation and their leaders, and it was in the chapel space that its propagation and defence was materially and symbolically located. Figure 4 shows us that by the end of the 1930s, however, the expression of Methodism in French had become limited in space to the chapels most removed from the urban centre of the island, and that by 1950, records indicate French had been essentially replaced. The spatial retreat of francophone Methodism followed changes amongst its members and in the island's society as a whole, with young people being in the vanguard of linguistic change.

It has been argued that the First World War, in addition to its profound social impact, served as a moment of linguistic watershed in both Jersey and Guernsey.[99] During the War, island Methodists were kept abreast of news of the fighting, with money collected at services and lectures used for humanitarian aid during the war effort,[100] and a number of Sunday school scholars donating the money that would have been spent on their prizes to assist Belgian refugees (Figure 6).[101] Local men, Methodists among them, returned to the island at the end of the War, having fought for Britain and experienced a prolonged contact with their fellow Britons, with British customs, British institutions and the English language. On Armistice Day, and at subsequent anniversaries, the island's chapels held services to commemorate the soldiers who fell during the War in common with chapels throughout Britain.[102] Such services combined solemnity and mourning with solidarity and patriotism, and the orders of service arrived pre-printed in English from mainland Britain, authorised for use by the Methodist Conference.[103] Free of French hymns, such services used English as a language suitable for divine supplication and praise.

With pastoral oversight affected by a number of Local Preachers leaving the island to fight, Methodist and other Nonconformist chapels were obliged to share services and preachers, and this was organised under the auspices of the Jersey Free Church Council (JFCC). This body of churches, established in 1898, was essentially an urban and anglophone organisation; the majority of its member churches being established in St Helier, as illustrated in Figure 7.[104] It had organised inter-denominational ministerial exchange since its foundation, and preaching plans on the French Wesleyan circuit from the years of the First World War show the inclusion of several Preachers and Ministers from other JFCC member churches scheduled to lead services in rural chapels.[105] The extension of such co-operation into the rural spaces of the French Wesleyan circuit must have had significant effects. Introducing English services at a time of heightened concern and patriotism for the British nation, with prayers for chapel members enlisted and fighting for the British Army, established the English language as an appropriate and necessary expression of the spiritual and temporal sentiments of the circuit's congregations at the time. Indeed, at St Martin's Methodist Church, Circuit Steward David Marrett writes that English services continued to grow in popularity after the cessation of hostilities, gradually coming to outnumber French services in the 1920s.[106]

Outside of the chapel walls, however, a major driver of change was becoming apparent. In light of the 1899 Compulsory Education Act, and the law for Free Education passed by the States in 1912,[107] during the War all children were attending primary school, wherein English was employed as the standard language of instruction.[108] Notwithstanding occasional difficulty in comprehension amongst Jèrriais-speaking rural children, the English language was present both in parish schools, where its usage was sanctioned by British government inspections, and in private schools, where many farmers sent their children with the expectation that they would attain the supposed advantages of anglophone ability.[109] Indeed, the role of education in propagating the shared use of a language, along with a shared sense of connected national identity has been argued for by scholars of Channel Island history as well as by social theorists such as Bourdieu.[110] Faced with groups of children habituated and confident in English, Sunday school leaders had to weigh their own attachment to the French language as *la langue de Dieu* with the growing practical expediency of delivering instruction in the English language.

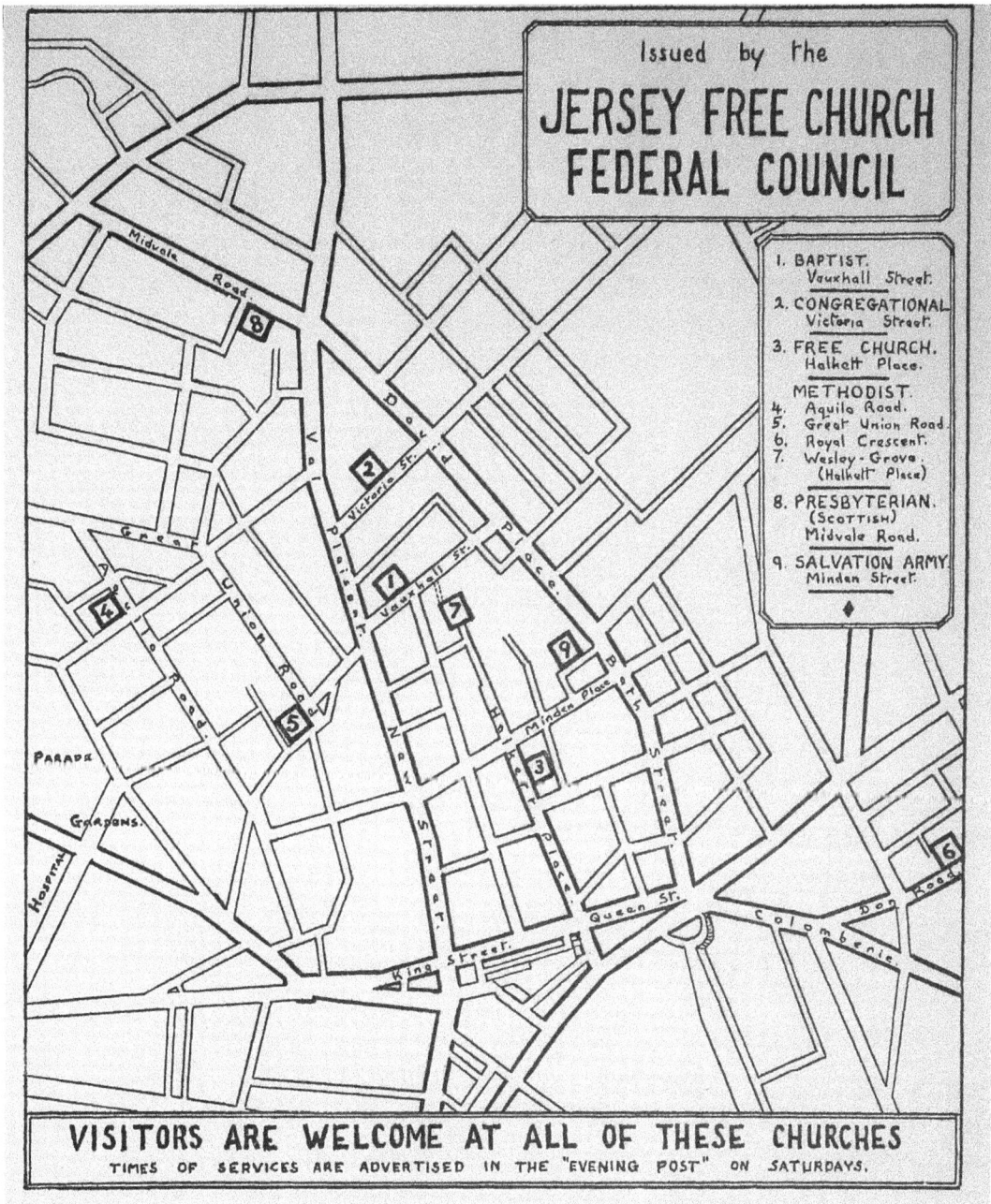

Figure 7: Location of member chapels of the Jersey Free Church Council in St Helier, Jersey (c. 1910)

J/C/AS/L/3 - *Jersey Heritage*

It is worthwhile considering the difference between the schoolroom and the chapel. Spatially, the two were adjacent, even in some cases attached, but symbolically the two remained separate. Though the Sunday school was a disciplined environment, and one in which Methodist doctrine and social conventions were propounded, it was not consecrated to divine service in the same manner as the chapel itself.[111] Where the French language was sanctioned, on divine, social and contractual bases in the chapel space, its usage in the schoolroom was, although customary, neither protected nor inevitable. Less resistant to change, therefore, the schoolroom would witness the more rapid transformation of its activities and its language in the 1920s and '30s.

The practice of Sunday scholars was directed and rewarded by a system of marks (*mérites*). If sufficient marks were attained, a prize would be given to the scholar, often before an audience of parents at a Sunday school anniversary.[112] In the 1920s, marks were typically awarded for punctuality, possession of Bible, completion of homework (where set), recitation of text, taking part in hymns, and good conduct (*'bonne conduite'*) in the schoolroom and the chapel.[113] Ordinances and deduction of marks also existed to regulate practice outside of and around the school room building, from loitering if arrived too early, to smoking, to the later limits of evening activities.[114] Young Methodists were thus trained in their behaviour just as they were trained in the doctrine of their faith. And Sunday scholars, 'wax to shape and marble to retain,'[115] were inducted and enrolled into wider Methodist concerns such as taking a pledge of abstinence from alcohol as part of the Band of Hope movement.[116] Disciplined morality was also a topic for discursive exhortation and admonishment. At the 1932 centenary celebrations for Les Frères Sunday School, the Reverend John du Feu delivered what was described as 'a stirring address in French, in which he appealed to the young men and women of the congregation to keep away from sin and temptation' – 'Young men and women,' he is recorded as saying, 'let your lives be pure...Do not go alone on the path of life, but take Jesus as your helper and guide.'[117]

The bodies and minds of young Methodists were sensitised, therefore, to both incentive and sanction, and directed by parental approval and ecclesial concern.[118] With the contemporaneous growth of English teaching in the island's primary schools, and the growing, though minority presence of English services in the chapel, Sunday schools became natural homes for the propagation of Methodist thought, doctrine and practice in the English language before this could become standard in the chapels themselves. Speech, as one practice amongst others, but one central to the expression of the Methodist faith, was delivered and trained by Sunday school leaders, and increasingly the words used were English. Furthermore, there was greater acceptance of and reliance on English materials and English doctrine for religious understanding. The Sunday school Leader, discharging the duties of *maître à parler* and thereby, perhaps, of *maître à penser*,[119] began to impart knowledge of English Methodism that through time served to ingrain a certain shared anglophone identity amongst the group.

The nature of the materials used in religious instruction in the Sunday school also changed as an expanded space of Methodist thought was being developed. A committee set up to consider a French translation of a newly revised catechism from Britain in 1925 advised the Sunday School Council of the now deprecated nature of cathechismal instruction and recitation, and recommended the cessation of such instruction to scholars under the age of nine.[120] It is possible to see, in these (adopted) recommendations that the resource of the catechism, a central part of the inherited doctrinal resources constitutive of francophone Methodism in Jersey, was gradually devalued both in its language and in the particular vision of Methodist faith it expounded. Where earlier generations of Methodist scholars had imbibed and repeated sections of the catechism, the reporting committee sought to expand the book's vision, and to transform its use into something 'interesting and useful' and more stimulating to 'the child mind'.[121] Such a concern with more active engagement with Methodist theology on the part of scholars, and eventually with the wider application of religion would continue to manifest itself into the 1930s.

Indeed, historians of Channel Island Methodism have argued that an intergenerational split emerged in the years up to and including the 1920s and early 1930s.[122] Played out throughout the circuit, chapels became loci of dispute between young people (and those who sought to retain them in the church), trained in an anglophone Methodism and whose first experiences of chapel services may have been under the leadership of monoglot British Ministers; and older members, spiritually and emotionally attached to a francophone expression of the Methodist faith that had been inherited from parents and grandparents and which had formed a part of the rural social networks they inhabited. 'Quite naturally', argued R. D. Moore, the younger generation preferred to attend English services, because 'they were more 'alive' and easier to understand' whilst parents and grandparents resisted, attached not only to the inherited, scriptural theology of Jersey Methodism, but to 'the language with which their deepest spiritual experiences were associated.'[123] At Ebenezer chapel in Trinity, Spence quotes the following personal communication from (Chapel member) Sir Arthur de la Mare:

> . . . it was only in the early twenties that any Methodist services in Trinity came to be conducted in English, much to the horror of many of the faithful, who regarded the use of English as a sort of blasphemy. Some of them actually boycotted services in the alien tongue.[124]

Viewing the chapel as a sacred space dedicated to francophone worship, and in the habit of worshipping in that language, older members could see the performance of the English language in that space as a sort of profane transgression. In absenting themselves from the chapel space whilst English services were held, these members symbolically resisted a vision of their social world that replaced French with English as *la langue de Dieu*. We may say that religious language was therefore implicated in a symbolic struggle for the 'production and imposition of the legitimate vision of the world' and of their place and identity within it.[125] And throughout the French Wesleyan circuit, the strong sense of collective identity was combined with the widely held individual attachment to, and sometimes stewardship of, one's own chapel in preventing amalgamation with other circuits.[126] So despite negotiations held between local Ministers, when the Wesleyan, Primitive and United (formerly Bible Christian) branches of Methodism joined to form one Methodist Church in 1932 (Figure 8 gives a sense of the importance of the occasion), Jersey's four circuits remained, at least on paper, separate.[127] Yet on the ground there was cooperation, with the common denominator of Ministers appointed by the Methodist Conference but expected to officiate within now relict denominational spaces in the island. [128]

In the face of such stasis, Ministers chose to project a show of movement, change, and inclusion within the national discourse of union. At a meeting in July 1933, the Superintendents of each of the island's four circuits collaborated to draw up a new Model Deed for each of the island's Methodist churches – indeed, for the new 'Methodist Church' – and made no mention of the role, privileged or otherwise, of the French language in the text.[129] In seeking to establish an equal constitutional footing for each of the Methodist circuits, and in displacing the nettlesome obstacle of the French language, they hoped to facilitate the delayed inception in the island of 'une seule et même Eglise, sous la designation "Methodist Church" en vertu de l'acte de Parlement intitulé "Methodist Church Union Act, 1929"...'[130] following what had occurred in mainland Britain. Furthermore, the proposed new united Methodist identity had been placed and performed in the island through the organisation of a celebratory parade and united service a few months earlier,[131] projecting an image of island Methodism as parallel to that of Britain, even if the actual situation remained tangential. In the archives it can be seen that the island's two newspapers had reported around 1,500 young Methodists proceeding from the People's Park through the streets of town on the 2nd of October 1932, carrying banners proclaiming union, and making 'a deep impression on spectators' on their way to the united service at Grove Place.[132] Therein, the Jersey Evening Post's reporter witnessed 'a magnificent pageant of youth', whose 'whole-hearted' hymnal performance led 'one [to feel] that union was after all a very real thing.'[133] Ministers propounded the arrival of union with little reported recognition of its retarded development in Jersey; one speaker 'gave explanations of the procedure adopted at the recent Conference at the Albert Hall and the signing of the Deed of Union, and then told his hearers that they should feel very proud they belonged to the largest and greatest Protestant Church in the world.'[134] Recreating the presence of Methodist Union in this way, the speaker sought to fashion amongst his young audience a collective sense of Methodist identity, a vision of the Methodist social world that was paraxial to that of their English Ministers. The service

Figure 8: Ministers attending the United Methodist Conference held in London, 1932.

J/C/AR/D/1 - *Jersey Heritage*

concluded with a valedictory performance of the hymn 'Onward Christian Soldiers' to the patriotic tune of 'Land of Hope and Glory'.[135] For those who organised the day's events, this was a further attempt to project the image of the island's Methodist faith, especially amongst its active youth membership, as irrevocably enjoined with the British nation.

Within the space of the Sunday school, therefore, young Methodist scholars were instructed in English, and in an anglophone Methodism, at variance with that of their parents and grandparents who had been trained in – and remained custodians of the capital of – francophone Methodism. On parade and at united services, moreover, these young people were conducted into highly visible performances of a fragile but growing British Methodist identity, through which Ministers sought to authorise and objectify the place of British, anglophone, and united Methodism within the island, despite the inherited circuit barriers that still, on paper at least, prevailed. Harvey *et al.* have argued for the importance of visible performance in fashioning sense of both identity and community,[136] and Bourdieu argues that such 'acts of theatricalization' are central to processes of objectification, constituting 'the conscious realization of the principles of division according to which these groups are objectively organised and through which the perception that they have of themselves is organized'.[137] Imagining themselves as members of a nationwide Methodist union, and even a worldwide Protestant community, young Jersey Methodists were developing a sense of identity far removed from that of inherited francophone insularity. And this was probably true of more than just their religious identity.

The modernising world

Throughout the 1920s and early 1930s, young Jersey Methodists were taught in such a way as to be positively disposed to the English language, a more socially-aware Methodist religious life, shared activity with other chapels and circuits, and a sense of Methodist identity in common with their counterparts in Britain. An age of progress in transport, communications and media,[138] the 1930s saw a generation of young Methodists trained in an anglophone faith reclaiming English services just as the island's society as a whole experienced more intercourse with mainland Britain, and perhaps a greater attachment to a sense of British identity, normatively expressed in English. Where new activities were performed that expanded spaces of Methodist thought and practice, modern, secular visions of the social world came to be widespread; and where the Second World War necessitated shared activity, the post-war environment facilitated circuit amalgamation. Established networks of rural, francophone Methodist performance, therefore, became fragmented, as social spaces converged and the geographical, as opposed to linguistic, organisation of religious space was privileged in Ministerial reasoning.

Having been trained in the discursive framework of, and invested with authority by, the British Methodist Conference, the Ministers who led Jersey's French Wesleyan circuit brought understandings of the Methodist faith to the island that were considerably different from those of the older Local Preachers. As the (now united) Methodist Church was politically involved with matters of social deprivation and the moral challenges of modernity in addition to personal matters of faith,[139] it may be supposed that its appointed Ministers brought a sensitivity to such discourses to their ministrations in the island. Evidence suggests that the scope of Jersey Methodist faith was changing, and that young people were placed in the vanguard of such change. Where groups such as the Association Chrétienne at Les Frères in 1907 had propounded local evangelisation along with prayer meetings and the distribution of religious texts,[140] in the 1920s and '30s groups such as the Wesley Guild and the newly formed Jersey Council of Young

Methodism (later Methodist Guild) were occupied both with concerns that had their provenance in the discourses of UK Methodism, such as peace, slums and Temperance, and with activities of a more secular nature. Chapters of this group, illustrated in Figure 2, held rallies, outdoor meetings, concerts in aid of national charities, lectures on topics of international interest and even sent representatives to the Young Methodism National Conference events in the UK.[141] The discourse of Temperance, in particular, became more pervasive throughout the circuit's chapels as they became more attuned to the matters that concerned Methodist chapels in the UK. The first order of business, for instance, for the Wesley Guild that had set up at Bethlehem Chapel in 1926 was to organise a Temperance evening.[142] Lectures on Temperance were held at other chapels, and Grove Place even hosted a visit of the British Women's Temperance Association for two years in a row.[143] Furthermore, the Wesley Guild and similar bodies facilitated a degree of mixing and group enjoyment that, although built upon a religious basis, was perhaps not solely aimed at personal spiritual development. New activities for the French Wesleyan circuit included table tennis, lantern lectures on diverse topics, concerts, literary evenings, suppers and visits to other branches of the Guild in the island.[144] Young people from other Christian denominations, and even groups unaffiliated to organised religion were invited to participate in some of the activities.[145] Through such varied programmes of activity, Methodism was engaging with everyday life beyond the scope of evangelisation, and Methodists themselves were interacting in contexts outside of the ecclesial (and nominally francophone) space of the chapel.

In many cases concomitant with such expansion in the networks of religious activity, young people in Jersey were mixing across social and geographical space to a greater degree. As the urban centre of St Helier became more important to the social life of the whole island, being both increasingly accessible and more frequently accessed, especially with the spread of motorised transport, the anglophone capital circulated therein came to be valued throughout more rural spaces. The movements of rural young people increasingly operated as the vectors of this change, bringing English to areas of rural life where Jersey-French or French had typically prevailed, such as the home, the farm and the parish hall.

The place of French, too, was changing. Once accepted without question as constitutive of Jersey identity, the language began to be associated with French people, and a number of supposedly negative concomitant cultural attributes. Breton immigration reached its peak at the turn of the twentieth century, and remained numerically important for several more decades, with thousands of seasonal labourers coming to the island mostly, but not solely, to work in agriculture.[146] Ministering to their spiritual needs were a number of Catholic Priests and Religious, with churches in town and country.[147] At variance with the established protestant rural social order,[148] and with the expansion of their religious expression limited by laws passed within a wider anti-Catholic discourse of the time,[149] French people and their francophone religion were considered alien to Jersey's society,[150] and the putative common bond of language may have served more to escalate the abandonment of French by local people than to facilitate any fruitful exchange.[151] Indeed, whilst some of the Breton labourers themselves sought to acquire English as 'la langue des maîtres', it has been argued that the majority of their children made rapid gains in the language, eager to assimilate into a Jersey society where English was considered the language of progress and success.[152] Finding itself increasingly displaced from the island's social order – the capital of its possession less and less valued within the context of a rapidly modernising British society – the French language was marginalized to perdurable formalities such as ceremonial addresses in the island's government.[153] Any sense of francophone identity was gradually negated as social, religious and educational apparatuses cleaved ever closer to the British model.

In every sense, the expression of the Methodist faith in Jersey was taking on a new inflection. By the late 1930s, the cadre of Circuit Ministers was made up entirely of anglophone men from the UK.[154] Where French services were still being held, they were led by Local Preachers who were becoming older and older. The generational gap mentioned in the last section was evident in that as these francophone Local Preachers retired or died, they were not being replaced by younger men with the same ability or desire to preach a Methodist theology in the French language.[155] As we have seen, this was because they had been trained according to different habits, in a different language and with different theological foci. Though some of them were bilingual, more generally the cultural capital of francophone Methodism had become less widely held and less valued in society.

Sharing an Occupied island

The Second World War had a profound impact on every aspect of Jersey society. As the only part of British soil to be occupied by German forces, the Channel Islands found themselves cut off from mainland Britain and besieged by a military enemy.[156] Some Ministers and a proportion of the Methodist community evacuated the island just before German forces landed; part of approximately 20% of the island's population that left before Occupation made it impossible.[157] Under such closed conditions, the symbolic barriers between different Methodist circuits, having already been transgressed quite habitually through the 1930s, dissolved quite rapidly, and the events of the years from 1940 to 1945 generally reflect a sharing of limited material and pastoral resources along with an expansion of the interaction between members already evident before the Occupation. A day-by-day chronicle of life during this period from the perspective of a young Methodist in the French circuit is provided in Nan Le Ruez's *Occupation Diary*; and other personal testimonies, as well as archival materials, are instructive.

Chapel services were popular, both with members and non-members, during this difficult period and were one of the few public gatherings that were freely permitted by the occupying forces.[158] Some of the Methodist Guild and similar meetings continued throughout the Occupation, though others were cancelled due to limitations of electricity provision, motorised transport, and the fact of curfew.[159] Solidarity between chapels was manifested in many ways, from denominational Ministerial exchange to communal effort in the face of increasingly scarce resources.[160] Solidarity with Britain and the Allied war effort was also widespread and deeply felt, with a number of local Methodist members fighting in Europe, and the prospect of liberation from German Occupation dependent on Allied victory.[161] Intercourse between local chapels and the British Methodist Connexion was, however, disrupted or entirely proscribed by war conditions, with money previously sent to Connexional funds being retained in Jersey; 'our British nation being at war'; and disruptions to some services and activities revealed a gradually established dependency on materials from mainland Britain.[162] Communications that did manage to reach the island from Britain, by means of the Red Cross, were greeted with delight and gratitude – 'It was quite thrilling to hear from headquarters'.[163]

Exaltation understandably accompanied delight and gratitude when the island was finally liberated by British troops on the 9th of May, 1945. United services of thanksgiving were held, and minute books record expressions of profound thanks to Ministers who remained in the island throughout, to the British forces for their liberating action, and to God for His protection throughout the Occupation.[164] The unprecedented degree of ecclesial and social interaction was combined with an acute interest and empathy with British affairs – perhaps even greater than that engendered by the First World War [165]– and led to the sustained effort towards amalgamation of all of the island's Methodist circuits in the post-bellum atmosphere of goodwill and co-operative action. In terms of language, it appears that only a very few French services were held throughout the Occupation, and the immediate post-war years have been cited as a great watershed period for Jèrriais, with many parents choosing not to pass the language on to their children. Once severed links with Britain and the world had been re-established, and the economy recovered some its strength, an array of opportunities for education, employment and travel presented themselves to local people, and proficiency in English was the necessary price of admission.[166] The value of French in ecclesial spaces therefore declined along with the value of Jèrriais in less formal spheres.[167] Indeed, those organising and reflecting upon circuit amalgamation would go on to argue that the language question, so thorny just a few decades earlier, had now been resolved.

SITUATION OF METHODIST CHURCHES IN JERSEY.

And Proposed division in scheme for Amalgamation.

St.Ouens

Bethlehem

Los Freres

Ebenezer

Carmel

Les Landes
X

①

②

③

Six Roads

St.Martins

Bethesda

Philadelphie

Sion

Air-
Port

Augres
⑤

Eden

Gorey

④

Galaad

First
Tower

St.Helier

⑥

Tabor

St.Aubin

⑧

Georgetown

Le
Rocque

⑦

Bethel

Samares

Aquila Rd.
X
Gt.Union Rd.

Grove
Place

Wesle

Harbour

Royal
Crescent X

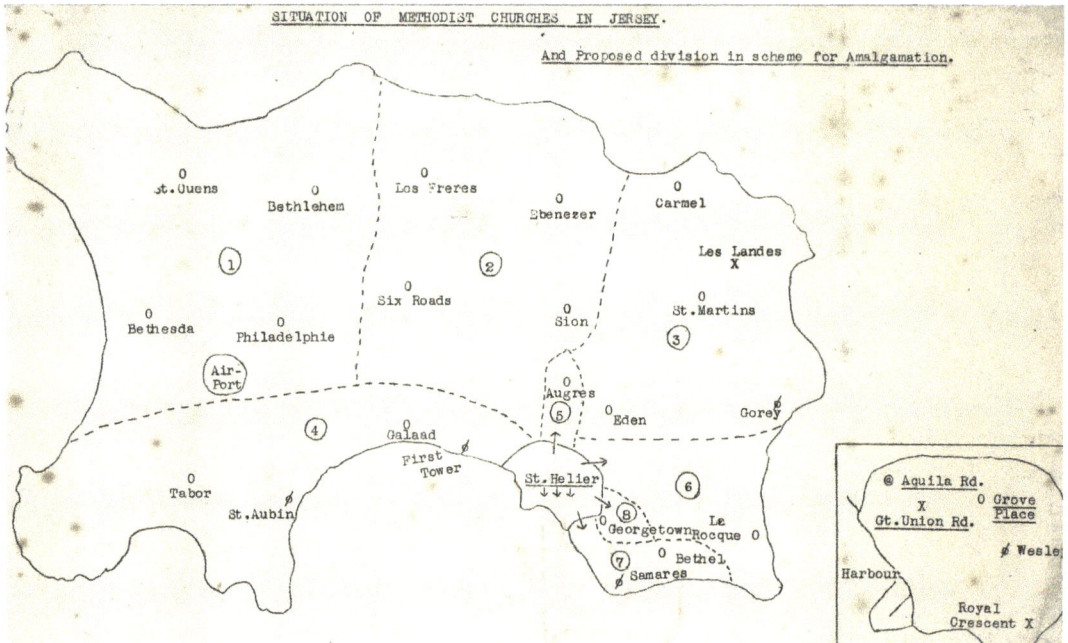

Figure 9: Sketch of the proposed division of Jersey at the time of circuit amalgamation, 1946

Lord Coutanche Library, Société Jersiaise

Amalgamation

The amalgamation negotiations that took place after the War built upon the interaction of years of shared services across circuit lines, as previously mentioned, but were also a continuation of occasional conversations about potential amalgamation that had been recorded, between the Wesleyan circuits at least, as early as 1918.[168] After the 1932 Methodist Union failed to translate to the structure of Jersey's Methodist circuits, the issue became more pressing. In 1931, the English Wesleyan circuit had passed a resolution stating that 'the vital needs of the island do not require four circuits',[169] and a later meeting of the Jersey Methodist Council had narrowly passed a vote to establish a committee to 'explore local union of Methodist circuits'.[170] Ministers and circuit leaders propounded a rationale for amalgamation, arguing that 'a re-distribution of the Ministers is essential' at an island scale and, *eo ipso*, 'for the future use of Ministerial service the churches should be so grouped as to make more concentration possible.'[171] The slow pace of change had caused frustration amongst its proponents, however, and a confidential, undated and unsigned letter sent to the Reverend Colin Roberts expresses the private belief that 'what can be done on the mainland in one year, needs at least, three on the island.'[172]

Indeed, nothing substantive was achieved before the outbreak of the Second World War, and it is only in December 1945, in anticipation of a special commission being sent from the British Methodist Conference the next year, that a potential scheme for amalgamation drawn up by the Reverend J. R. Rider was discussed by the Jersey Methodist Island Committee.[173] The scheme itself was modified at subsequent meetings, as individual circuits expressed their reservations, but a Jersey Amalgamation Committee decided in April 1946, days before the arrival of the Conference Commission, to go ahead with plans for amalgamation as shown on Figure 9.[174]

This proposed new geography of Methodism in the island prioritised proximity and efficient ministerial oversight over circuit affiliation. It can be seen from this map (Figure 9) that hitherto solely English language chapels were joined with chapels from the French circuit; urban chapels such as Wesley were concatenated with rural ones such as Bethel, and in the north-east of the island, three parishes and three circuits were combined in one section of the new Methodist organisation. The proposed scheme met with the approval of the visiting Commission, who expressed the hope 'without any wish to dictate' that amalgamation along these lines 'will prove to be practicable'.[175] Even with the surprise withdrawal of the Aquila Road and Great Union Road circuits,[176] the two Wesleyan circuits, separated for generations by language, adopted the scheme with minor changes.[177] On August the 27th, 1947, the *Jersey Morning News* announced the achievement of Methodist amalgamation in a victorious tone, asserting:

> The remarkable extent to which English has ousted French as the language commonly used in Jersey is illustrated in the history of the Grove Place and Wesley Methodist circuits, to be re-united on September 7th.[178]

The matter of language was cited thereafter in terms of facilitation. Amalgamation was possible in light of the recent 'absence of purely French Ministrations' read the Quarterly Letter published in the first Wesley Grove Circuit Plan;[179] 'The old language difficulties no longer exist' stated Reverend Rider in the 1947 centenary booklet of Grove Place Chapel.[180] It was also stressed that the union was in fact a re-union, reflecting the resolution of circumstances of linguistic difference that had led to the original division of the island into separate circuits in the nineteenth century.[181] It was considered, therefore, that:

> No feature of our Methodist life in the amalgamating churches makes it impossible for the new circuit to enjoy the fruits of full communion with one another in Church life and in Christian service to the community committed to our spiritual care.[182]

Amalgamation was complete; the French Wesleyan circuit was no more, and, notwithstanding infrequent French services and commemorative francophone evenings in the following years,[183] the ecclesial expression of francophone

Methodism in Jersey had come to an end. Indeed, French was now considered in many quarters as a foreign language.[184] The new amalgamated Methodism in Jersey was organised according to proximity in geographical space and ease of ministerial oversight instead of according to the groups assembled in social space around shared resources of cultural capital. Where, only twenty years earlier, senior chapel members were boycotting English services, now anglophone Methodism was a *fait accompli*.

Figure 10: Postcard of the Georgetown Methodist Chapel, 1909.   J/C/BU/3 - *Jersey Heritage*

Figure 11: Georgetown Methodist Chapel, 2009.   *Rory Hill*

Conclusion

The decline in the expression of francophone Methodism in Jersey entailed a closely connected network of social and cultural factors. In this short study it can be seen how changes in doctrine and training, in circuit spaces, in social activity, and in the place of language in Jersey society were all linked to its decline and eventual displacement.

In Jersey, from the turn of the twentieth century, francophone Methodism was intimately linked with rural life and landscape through activities such as Sunday school outings and open-air preaching, and through the networks of its members in the country parishes; and French was recognised as the appropriate language for use in ecclesial space – *la langue de Dieu*. The Methodist message expressed in such space was inflected with the character of its surrounding, and antecedent, rural society, with written materials, hymns and oral sermons and exhortations valued amongst the symbolic capital of the French Wesleyan circuit.

The continued value of francophone Methodist capital was, however, contested in the light of discourses of Britishness that grew rapidly from around the time of the First World War, and training of young people in the English language that had spread widely from the turn of the century. Symbolic struggles took place over the pulpit and the chapel space, as errancy in language was policed like errancy in doctrine. Under pressure from within and without, however, such resistance could not prevail, and the sacred place of the French language began to be transgressed in a spatial and temporal pattern that reached the most isolated rural chapels last. Where some older Methodists saw the replacement of the French language with English as a kind of profane transgression, young people were enjoined more easily in the change as they had been raised in the latter language and in the wider social and theological scope of British Methodism, and they had taken leading parts in public performances of a new British Methodist identity.

From the 1930s onwards, the spatial networks of these young Methodists developed linguistic connections different from those of previous generations, and the urban space of town was encompassed in both social and geographical terms. The French language underwent a discursive change from conflation with local, rural identity, to connotations of national and religious foreignness, and the pressures and necessary co-operation of the wartime Occupation solidified a consciously British identity amongst the island's population as well as solidarity amongst churches. In the light of shared social experiences and religious expression, therefore, amalgamation of Jersey's Methodist circuits took place, as the practical logic of material proximity was valorised over the cultural worth of linguistic separation, and the French language lost its value and use within a transformed religious landscape.

The analysis undertaken in this study comes from a particular cultural and historical geographical perspective, and draws upon certain theoretical ideas which other writers may not use. Whilst these ideas are not essential to historical work, they have helped to interpret and narrate the process of transformation in language which may be seen as inextricably related to social and cultural transformations in island life and to doctrinal and practical transformations in the Methodist Church. That Church remains a living institution, with chapels and members spread throughout the island. Its buildings remain in many cases as beautiful and sturdy as they would have appeared to Victorian and Edwardian islanders (consider Figures 10 and 11), and some retain French inscriptions inside or out. The Church has also left behind numerous and detailed archival records which allow historians and other scholars to examine its history and how that relates to the wider human story of the island. As argued in the introduction to this study, examining the connection of language and religion offers us the chance to better understand an aspect of social history that is intimately related to identity, belonging and community. Indeed, given the abundance of material that is available to us in archives and libraries, there is also the potential to excavate the history of language change in other island institutions – such as the Anglican Church, to take one comparable example – and thereby to better understand what is at stake when one language gives way to another, but when faith remains.

Figure 12: Sunday scholars and their parents from Philadelphie Chapel at a Sunday School outing in July 1913. Picture published in the Jersey Morning News of July 19th, 1913, with the following caption:

'The children attending Philadelphie (Wesleyan) Sunday School held their annual driving picnic yesterday afternoon. The party, accommodated in eleven vans, left St. Peter's Post Office at about 1:30, and after a pleasant drive through the country, reached the western side of Rozel, where tea was served in a specially erected marquee. A start on the return journey was made at about 8:30pm'

SJPA/049136 - *Percival Dunham, Société Jersiaise Photographic Archive*

Figure 13: Sunday scholars from Philadelphie chapel about to take part in a race during their Sunday school outing, July 1913

SJPA/049137 - *Percival Dunham, Société Jersiaise Photographic Archive*

Figure 14: Sunday scholars and Rechabites (members who had taken a pledge of abstinence from alcohol) from Grove Place chapel preparing to depart on a Sunday school outing, 1914

SJPA/049534 - *Percival Dunham, Société Jersiaise Photographic Archive*

Figure 15: Four new ministers of the French Wesleyan Methodist Circuit in front of Grove Place Chapel, 1914

SJPA/049614 - *Percival Dunham, Société Jersiaise Photographic Archive*

Figure 16: Some of the Guernsey visitors and local delegates to the Channel Islands Wesleyan Synod taken outside Grove Place chapel, May 1914

SJPA/049012 - *Percival Dunham, Société Jersiaise Photographic Archive*

Figure 17: View of the parades and celebrations at People's Park, St Helier on Coronation Day, 1911. Note people carrying the banner 'Ecole Wesleyenne'

SJPA/032566 - *Francis Foot, Société Jersiaise Photographic Archive*

Notes

1 See: F. Guiton, *Histoire du Méthodisme Wesleyen dans les Iles de la Manche*, London, John Mason, 1846; M. Le Lièvre, *Histoire du Méthodisme dans les Iles de la Manche 1784-1884*, Paris, Librairie Evangélique, 1885; H. Arnett, *Handbook of Methodist history in Jersey*, Jersey, Jersey Evening Post, 1909; R. D. Moore, *Methodism in the Channel Islands*, London, Epworth Press, 1952; G. R. Morley, *The story of Methodism at St. Aubin, Jersey*, Jersey, Trustees of St Aubin Methodist Church/Bennett Brothers, 1967; Anonymous, *Bicentenary of Methodism in Jersey, Channel Islands 1774-1974*, Jersey, JEP Publications, 1974; D. Marett, *Chapelle Wesleyenne 1851-2001: Celebrating the one hundred and fiftieth anniversary of St Martin's Methodist Chapel*, Jersey, Les Rues, 2000.

2 Moore, *Methodism in the Channel Islands*, op.cit., p.100.

3 R. Lemprière, *History of the Channel Islands*, London, Robert Hale, 1980, p.20-21.

4 P. Stevens, *Victor Hugo in Jersey*, Chichester, Phillimore, 2002, p.33-34; L. J. Marr, *History of the Bailiwick of Guernsey*, London, Phillimore, 1982, p.272; Lemprière, *History of the Channel Islands*, op. cit., p.180-81.

5 English was also the language of instruction for the young women of Guernsey, with the founding of the Ladies' College in 1872; and of Jersey in 1880, where the Jersey Ladies' College was founded by a group of Methodists from Grove Place.

6 Universal education delivered in English beginning in the early twentieth century was a significant part of this change, and will be mentioned later in the text. In the matter of government, it should be noted that the correspondence of the Lieutenant-Governor, the representative of the Crown in the island, has generally always been in English, as have the orders given to British troops stationed in the island from time to time.

7 'Il n'est pas très facile de préciser le moment où la branche française s'est séparée de la branche anglaise dans chaque île...il semble que la séparation se fit graduellement.' Le Lièvre, *Histoire du Méthodisme dans les Iles de la Manche*, op. cit., p.432-33. '[I]t seems almost impossible to say when the division really did come about...' Arnett, *Handbook of Methodist history in Jersey*, op.cit., p.44.

8 Arnett, *Handbook of Methodist history in Jersey*, op.cit., p.54.

9 The Bible Christian Church separated from the Wesleyan Church in 1815, under the leadership of the Cornishman William O'Bryan. The Primitive Methodist Church was established in 1811 under the leadership of Hugh Bourne and William Clowes. Both Churches grew and spread overseas, and both eventually re-united with the Methodist Church in the twentieth century.

10 Moore, *Methodism in the Channel Islands*, op.cit., p.104.

11   Arnett, *op.cit.*, p.71; Moore, *Methodism in the Channel Islands, op.cit.*, pp.112-13; see also *Wesley Grove Circuit Coronation Souvenir Directory Membership Roll, 1953*, J/C/F/E/1, Methodist Collection, Jersey Archive.

12   See, for example: M. Pacione, The relevance of religion for a relevant human geography *Scottish Geographical Journal* 115 (1999) pp.117-31; M. Gilsenan, *Recognizing Islam: religion and society in the modern Middle East*, London, I. B. Tauris, 2000; S. Naylor and J. R. Ryan, The Mosque in the suburbs: negotiating religion and ethnicity in south London *Social and Cultural Geography* 3 (2002) pp.39-59; L. Kong, In search of permanent homes: Singapore's House Churches and the politics of space *Urban Studies* 39 (2002) pp.1573-86; A. Ivakhiv, Toward a geography of "religion": mapping the distribution of an unstable signifier *Annals of the Association of American Geographers* 96 (2006) pp.169-75; R. Jones, Sacred cows and thumping drums: claiming territory as 'zones of tradition' in British India *Area* 39 (2007) pp.55-65; S. Mills, Duty to God/my Dharma/Allah/Waheguru: diverse youthful religiosities and the politics and performance of informal worship *Social and Cultural Geography* 13 (2012) pp.481-99; S. D. Brunn and D. A. Gilbreath, *The changing world religion map: sacred places, identities, practices and politics*, Amsterdam, Springer, 2015; A. Maddrell and R. Scriven, Celtic pilgrimage, past and present: from historical geography to contemporary embodied practices *Social and Cultural Geography* 17 (2016) pp.300-321.

13   L. Kong, Mapping 'new' geographies of religion: politics and poetics in modernity *Progress in Human Geography* 25 (2001) pp.211-33; L. Kong, Religious Landscapes in J. S. Duncan, N. Johnson and R. H. Schein eds., *A Companion to Cultural Geography*, Oxford, Blackwell, 2008, pp.365-81.

14   C. Brace, A. R. Bailey and D. C. Harvey, Religion, place and space: a framework for investigating historical geographies of religious identities and communities *Progress in Human Geography* 30 (2006) pp.28-43.

15   Brace, Bailey and Harvey, Religion, place and space, *op.cit.*, p.38.

16   D. Harvey, C. Brace and A. Bailey, Parading the Cornish subject: Methodist Sunday schools in West Cornwall, c.1830-1930 *Journal of Historical Geography* 33 (2007) pp.24-44; A. R. Bailey, D. C. Harvey and C. Brace, Disciplining youthful Methodist bodies in nineteenth-Century Cornwall *Annals of the Association of American Geographers* 97 (2007) pp.142-57.

17   Brace, Bailey and Harvey, *op.cit.*, p.36.

18   J. Fishman, *The sociology of language: an interdisciplinary social science approach to language in society*, Rowley MA, Newbury House, 1972; E. Hobsbawm and T. Ranger eds., *The invention of tradition*, Cambridge, Cambridge University Press, 1983; B. Anderson, *Imagined communities: reflections on the origin and spread of nationalism*, London, Verso, 1991.

19   C. Withers, *Gaelic in Scotland 1698-1891: the geographical history of a language*, Edinburgh, John Donald Publishers, 1983; J. Morrissey, Contours of colonialism: Gaelic Ireland

and the early colonial subject *Irish Geography* 37 (2004) pp.88-102; W. McLeod and J. Smith, Resistance to monolinguality: The languages of Scotland since 1918, in I. Brown, T. O. Clancy, S. Manning, M. Pittock, K. Horvat and A. Hales, *The Edinburgh history of Scottish literature: modern transformations: new identities (from 1918)*, Edinburgh, Edinburgh University Press, 2006, pp.21-30.

20   D. Ryon, Cajun French, sociolinguistic knowledge, and language loss in Lousiana *Journal of Language, Identity and Education* 1 (2002) pp.279-93; L. Oakes, French: a language for everyone in Québec? *Nations and Nationalism* 10 (2004) pp.539-58; R-M. Crossan, The retreat of French from Guernsey's public primary schools, 1800-1939 *Transactions of the Société Guernesiaise* 25 (2006) pp.851-88.

21   R. Hill, *Circuits of capital: placing the end of francophone Methodism in Jersey, 1900-1950*, Unpublished BSc thesis, University of Exeter, 2010.

22   G. Williams, *Religion, language and nationality in Wales*, Cardiff, University of Wales Press, 1979; C. W. J. Withers, Highland clubs and chapels: Glasgow's Gaelic community in the eighteenth century *Scottish Geographical Magazine* 101 (1985) pp.16-27; F. MacDonald, Towards a spatial theory of worship: some observations from Presbyterian Scotland *Social and Cultural Geography* 3 (2002) pp.61-80; R. M. O. Pritchard, Protestants and the Irish language: historical heritage and current attitudes in Northern Ireland *Journal of Multilingual and Multicultural Development* 25 (2004) pp.62-82; N. M. Wolf, *An Irish-speaking island: state, religion, community, and the linguistic landscape in Ireland, 1770-1870*, Madison WI, University of Wisconsin Press, 2014; But see also: J-L. Marfany, Religion and the survival of 'minority' languages: the Catalan case *Social History* 30 (2005) p.155-74; J. K. H. Tse, Making a Cantonese-Christian family: quotidian habits of language and background in a transnational Hongkonger church *Population, Space and Place* 17 (2011) pp.756-78.

23   P. Bourdieu, *Language and symbolic power*, Cambridge, Polity Press, 1991.

24   These ideas are also developed in Bourdieu's other works: P. Bourdieu, *Outline of a theory of practice*, Cambridge, Cambridge University Press, 1977; P. Bourdieu, *Distinction: a social critique of the judgment of taste*, London, Routledge, 1984; P. Bourdieu, *The social structures of the eonomy*, Cambridge, Polity Press, 2005.

25   R. Hill, *Circuits of capital, op. cit.*

26   Minute of the meeting held on September 6th 1934, *Grove Place Circuit Local Preachers Meeting Minutes, 1910-1946*, J/C/D/A/5, Methodist Collection, Jersey Archive. See also: Minute of the meeting held on July 12th 1932, *Grove Place Chapel Trust Minute Book*, J/C/W/A/3, Methodist Collection, Jersey Archive; Minute of the meeting held on July 13th 1938, *Minute Book for the Sunday School Council at Carmel Chapel, 1886-1963*, J/C/M/A/3, Methodist Collection, Jersey Archive.

27   On the drafting of laws in English in the early twentieth century see, for example, G. Price, French in the Channel Islands, in G. Price (ed.) *Languages in Britain and Ireland*, Oxford, Blackwell, 2000, pp.187-196.

28   Plans of Services held in the French Circuit, J/C/D/E/7 – J/C/D/E/51, Methodist Collection, Jersey Archive. NB It is of course possible that not all services in a particular language were annotated as such on the plan.

29   The data for this map were taken from: *Membership Schedule, 1938*, J/C/BB/A/1, Methodist Collection, Jersey Archive.

30   The data for this map are the dates of the first English minutes recorded in the Trustees' Minute Books of the chapels of the French Wesleyan Circuit, held in the Methodist Collection at the Jersey Archive. Where these minute books are not available for a particular chapel, dates of the first English entries in other materials such as Leaders' Minutes or Trustees' Accounts are taken instead, or estimates are made based on two or more of these materials where there is a disparity. Such dates are in parentheses on the map.

31   The data for this map were taken from the Plans of Services (Quarterly Preaching Plans) for the French Wesleyan Circuit held in the Methodist Collection at the Jersey Archive. Reference numbers: J/C/D/E/9, J/C/D/E/14, J/C/D/E/19, J/C/D/E/24, J/C/D/E/29, J/C/D/E/34, J/C/D/E/36, J/C/D/E/39, J/C/D/E/43-51. The total number of services in a year varies per chapel and according to the calendar, but may be taken to be 52 as a minimum, i.e. the number of Sundays in a year. It should also be noted that the annotation of 'A' for English services and 'F' for French services on the Preaching Plans may not have been applied consistently.

32   J. D. Kelleher, *The triumph of the country: rural community in nineteenth-century Jersey*, Dublin, John Appleby Publishing, 1994; N. C. W. Spence, *A brief history of Jèrriais*, Jersey, Le Don Balleine, 1993; G. Kempson, *Language death: Jèrriais, a case in point? A geolinguistic study of minority language decline*, Unpublished thesis, Southampton University, 1991.

33   These two terms will be used throughout this study to refer to the same Jersey Norman French language.

34   See also: A. Gilles, *The influence of Nos Iles: a symposium on the Channel Islands on the shaping of the future of Jersey after the Second World War*, Unpublished Master's thesis, Université de Caen, 1995, p.5.

35   H. Johnson, Localising Jersey through song *Shima: The International Journal of Research into Island Cultures* 2 (2008) pp.73-98, p.89; Spence, *op. cit.*; Kempson, *op.cit.*; C. Fleury and H. Johnson, Le phénomène de revitalisation culturelle à Jersey: un exemple d'accompagnement symbolique à la mondialisation, *Annales de Géographie* 690 (2013) pp.200-219.

36   Kelleher, *op.cit.*, p.134.

37   Entry for March 19th 1920, *Bethel Chapel Accounts Book, 1894-1996*, J/C/K/B/3, Methodist Collection, Jersey Archive; Minute of the meeting held on January 20th 1909, *Salem Chapel Trust Minute Book, 1867-1923*, J/C/AG/A/1, Methodist Collection,

Jersey Archive; *Programme for a Drama Production performed by the Wesleyan school at La Rocque Chapel*, Undated (c. 1909), J/C/X/C/4, Methodist Collection, Jersey Archive.

38   Bailey, Harvey and Brace, Disciplining youthful Methodist bodies, *op.cit.*; Harvey, Brace and Bailey, Parading the Cornish subject, *op.cit.*

39   Entries for July 13th 1907 and August 2nd 1914, *Bethel Chapel Accounts Book, op.cit.*

40   Minutes of the meetings held on 30th June 1922 and 18th June 1924, *Georgetown Chapel Sunday School Minute Book, 1919-1936*, J/C/T/A/2, Methodist Collection, Jersey Archive.

41   Minute of the meeting held on 31st August 1915, *Register of the Committee for Sunday School at Bethlehem Chapel, 1872-1926*, J/C/L/B/1, Methodist Collection, Jersey Archive.

42   W. Jenkins, Between the lodge and the meeting-house: mapping Irish Protestant identities and social worlds in late Victorian Toronto *Social & Cultural Geography* 4 (2003) p.75-98.

43   Brace, Bailey and Harvey, Religion, place and space, *op.cit.*

44   'Open Air Campaign', *Plan of Services held in the French Circuit, May-September 1925*, J/C/D/E/29, Methodist Collection, Jersey Archive.

45   D. Carter, *A Jersey childhood*, Jersey, CTV Publications, 1989.

46   Lord (A.) Coutanche, A glance at the past ninety years *Annual Bulletin of the Société Jersiaise* 18 (1964) pp. 401-4; J. Likeman, Ecole Elementaire or Elementary School *Annual Bulletin of the Société Jersiaise* 25 (1991) pp.501-11; Kelleher, *op.cit.*; C. Hublart, *Le français de Jersey* Unpublished thesis, Université de l'Etat à Mons: Ecole d'Interprètes Internationaux, 1978; cf. L. Ozanne, *A journey Through faith*, Guernsey, Melody Press, 2006.

47   It is interesting to read Jean de Quetteville's words a hundred years previous to this, when considering the case of a Local Preacher from Guernsey, Jean de Putron, and the trouble he had preaching amongst French speakers in Canada given the strong influence of his Guernsey-French. '*Notre ami de Putron avait étudié la langue française et considérablement amélioré son style et sa prononciation avant de quitter l'île ; mais, par ce qu'il en dit, il est aisé de voir qu'un prédicateur, quel que fut son zèle et ses talents, ne pourrait rien faire en pays français, à moins de s'être préalablement défait du patois et de l'accent de nos îles.*' *Magasin Méthodiste*, 1817, p.91 ; cited in Le Lièvre, *op. cit.*, p.474.

48   N. C. W. Spence, Le sort de la francophonie à Jersey *Revue de l'Avranchin et du Pays de Granville* 78 (2001) pp.165-77, p.172.

49   A. D. Gilbert, Methodism, dissent and political stability in early industrial England *Journal of Religious History* 10 (1979) pp.387-99, p.384, cited in Brace *et al., op.cit.*

50   D. Hempton, *Methodism: empire of the spirit*, New Haven CT, Yale University Press, 2005, p.80.

51   O. Riis, The role of religion in legitimating the modern structuration of society *Acta Sociologica* (1989) pp.137-53, pp.147-8.

52   Cf. J. Waller ed., *A Methodist pilgrimage in France: the journal of Matthew Gallienne*, Loughborough, Loughborough University Press, 1989, pp.17-18.

53   Kelleher, *op.cit.*, p.118-19.

54   Hempton, *Methodism, op.cit.*; D. M. Chapman, *Born in song: Methodist worship in Britain*, Warrington, Church in the Market Place Publications, 2006.

55   This phenomenon has been noted by Kelleher, *op.cit.*, p.119; and by F. Le Poidevin, *Les Capelles Methodist Church: the story of 200 years 1786-1986*, Guernsey, Les Capelles Methodist Church Family Committee/Melody Press, 1986, p.31.

56   Moore, *Methodism in the Channel Islands, op.cit.*, p.112.

57   *Souvenir Quotation Book for the French Wesleyan Circuit*, 1909, J/C/D/H/5, Methodist Collection, Jersey Archive; *Souvenir Quotation Book issued in connection with the Les Frères Chapel Bazaar*, 1912, J/C/Z/J/2, Methodist Collection, Jersey Archive.

58   Minute of the meeting held on the 19th of March 1900, *Grove Place Circuit Local Preachers (Predicateurs Locaux) Minute Book*, J/C/D/A/1, Methodist Collection, Jersey Archive.

59   Anonymous, *Newscutting relating to the centenary celebrations of Les Frères Chapel Sunday school*, 1932, J/C/Z/G/2 Methodist Collection, Jersey Archive; Anonymous, *Anniversary of St Ouen's Chapels*, 1921, Document 9 Methodism Box File, Lord Coutanche Library, Société Jersiaise (Jersey); Bethesda Chapel, 'Avant-Propos', *Bethesda Chapel Secretarial Minute Book*, 1872-1967, J/C/K/A/1 Methodist Collection, Jersey Archive; P. E. Brée, *The Origin and Development of Methodism in La Rocque*, 1932, J/C/X/F/2 Methodist Collection, Jersey Archive; Cf. Chapman, *Born in song, op. cit.*, p.327.

60   Moore, *op. cit.*

61   K. Cracknell and S. J. White, *An introduction to world Methodism*, Cambridge, Cambridge University Press, 2005, pp.194-95.

62   Kelleher, *op. cit.*; A. Gilles, *The influence of Nos Iles, op. cit.*

63   K. F. Broughton, *Methodism and an island community: Jersey 1770-1870*, Unpublished thesis, Jersey Library Local Studies section, 1995, p.110-12; C. G. Stevens, *The vanished chapels and priories of Jersey*, Unpublished manuscript, Société Jersiaise, 1977; cf. Le Poidevin, *Les Capelles, op. cit.*, p.1 ; R. C. Zachmann, John Calvin (1509-1564) in C. Lindberg (ed.), *The Reformation theologians: an introduction to theology in the Early Modern period*, Oxford, Blackwell, 2002, pp.184-97.

64   L. Mourant, *History of Eden Chapel*, 1983, p.4, J/C/P/E/1, Methodist Collection, Jersey Archive.

65   Broughton, Methodism and an island community, *op. cit.*, pp.110-12.

66   Moore, *op. cit.*, p.112.

67   Moore, *op. cit.*, p.76. Some, of course, would translate French language materials into English, and vice-versa, mediating the two influences in Methodist expression.

68   Chapman, *op. cit.*; Hempton, *op. cit.*; Cracknell and White, *op. cit.*

69   Chapman, *op. cit.*, p.292.

70   Moore, *op. cit.*; Kelleher, *op. cit.*, p.119; Marett, *Chapelle Wesleyenne, op. cit.*

71   Y. Le Petit, Le Psautier Huguenot aux Iles Anglo-Normandes *Bulletin de la recherche sur le Psautier huguenot – Pandémonium pour l'Etude et la Prospection du Psautier* 9 (1994) pp.209-16, p.209.

72   Brace *et al.*, *op. cit.*, p.29-30 ; Kong, Mapping 'new' geographies of religion, *op. cit.*, pp.226-28.

73   Chapman, *op. cit.*, p.338.

74   MacDonald, Towards a spatial theory of worship, *op. cit.*

75   MacDonald, *op. cit.*, p.71.

76   Bourdieu, *Language and symbolic power, op. cit.*, p.138.

77   Minute of a meeting held on September 26th 1903, *Grove Place Circuit Quarterly Meeting Minutes, 1886-1940*, J/C/D/A/2, Methodist Collection, Jersey Archive. Conference was responsible for appointing Ministers to British Methodist circuits in general.

78   Minutes of meetings held on January 2nd and March 26th 1904, *Grove Place Circuit Quarterly Meeting Minutes, 1886-1940, op. cit.*

79   Minute of a meeting held on December 31st 1904, *Grove Place Circuit Quarterly Meeting Minutes, 1886-1940, op. cit.*

80   Minute of the meeting held on August 24th 1906, *Grove Place Chapel Trust Minute Book, 1845-1924*, J/C/W/A/1, Methodist Collection, Jersey Archive. Reverend Ernest Ewart Dewhurst born 1874 Preston, Lancashire; married Lily Shortland; they had two daughters, one born in Jersey. He died in London in 1947.

81   Minutes of the meetings held on February 22nd and September 14th 1906, *Grove Place Chapel Trust Minute Book, 1845-1924, op. cit.*

82   Minute of the meeting held on August 24th 1906, *Grove Place Chapel Trust Minute Book, 1845-1924, op. cit.*

83   Newscutting from *La Nouvelle Chronique de Jersey* relating to a meeting by the French Wesleyan Circuit held on the subject of 'English or French Language?', 1906, J/C/AL/G/1, Methodist Collection, Jersey Archive.

84   Newscutting from *La Nouvelle Chronique de Jersey, op. cit.*

85   Newscutting from *La Nouvelle Chronique de Jersey, op. cit.*

86   After Bourdieu, *Language and symbolic power, op. cit.*, pp. 248-49; p.111.

87   Cf. MacDonald, Towards a spatial theory of worship, *op. cit.*, pp.69-70.

88   Minute of the meeting held on December 7th 1906, *Grove Place Chapel Trust Minute Book, 1845-1924, op. cit.*

89   *Ibid.*

90   *Ibid.*

91   Minute of the meeting held on April 13th 1907, *Grove Place Circuit Local Preachers (Predicateurs Locaux) Minute Book, 1885-1910*, J/C/D/A/1, Methodist Collection, Jersey Archive.

92   Moore, *op. cit.*, p.133.

93   Minute of the meeting held on April 13th 1907, *op. cit.*

94   *Ibid.*

95   *Ibid.*

96   Minute of the meeting held on June 29th 1907, *Grove Place Circuit Quarterly Meeting Minutes, 1886-1940, op. cit.*

97   After Bourdieu, *op. cit.*, p.116.

98   Bourdieu, *op. cit.*, p.75.

99   Marett, *op. cit.*; Hublart, *op. cit.*; Crossan, *op. cit.*; Newscutting of an article from the *Guernsey Evening Press*, June 15th 1948, Scrapbook containing newscuttings relating to Methodist news, activities, members and Chapels, J/C/BQ/2, Methodist Collection, Jersey Archive.

100   *Sion Chapel Sunday School Order of Service and Song Sheet*, March 18th 1915, J/C/AK/G/2, Methodist Collection, Jersey Archive; Minute of the meeting held on the 31st of August 1915, *Register of the Committee for Sunday School at Bethlehem Chapel, 1872-1926*, J/C/L/B/1, Methodist Collection, Jersey Archive.

101   Certificates from the Wesleyan Methodist Sunday School, Wesley Street Chapel, 1915, J/C/BN/A/1, Methodist Collection, Jersey Archive.

102   *Roll of Honour of Wesleyan Methodist Sailors, Soldiers and Airmen who died from June 1917 until the close of the War, 1920*, J/C/BA/A/1, Methodist Collection, Jersey Archive.

103   *Form of Service for a Day of Solemn Prayer on behalf of the Empire and its Allies, for use during the First World War, 31st October 1915*, J/C/BA/B/1, Methodist Collection, Jersey Archive.

104   *Minute Book of the Executive committee of the Jersey Free Church Council, 1898-1911,* J/C/AS/A/3, Methodist Collection, Jersey Archive.

105   Minute Book of the Executive committee of the Jersey Free Church Council, 1898-1911, *op. cit.*; Plans of Services held in the French Wesleyan Circuit, 1915, J/C/D/E/19, Methodist Collection, Jersey Archive.

106   Marett, *Chapelle Wesleyenne, op. cit.*

107   Cf. States of Jersey, *Law on Primary Instruction in the States of Jersey,* 1912, J/C/AF/E/1, Methodist Collection, Jersey Archive.

108   Spence, *A brief history of Jèrriais, op. cit.,* p.8; cf. Hublart, *op. cit.,* p.42.

109   Kempson, *op. cit.,* p.22-23; Likeman, *op. cit.,* p.511.

110   Crossan, *op. cit.;* Bourdieu, *op. cit.,* pp.43-65; M. de Certeau, *Culture in the plural,* Minneapolis, University of Minnesota Press, p.86.

111   Chapman, *op. cit.,* p.321.

112   Carter, *A Jersey Childhood, op. cit.,* p.32.

113   Minute of the meeting held on June 30th 1922, *Georgetown Chapel Sunday School Minute Book, 1919-36,* J/C/T/A/2, Methodist Collection, Jersey Archive; 'Reglements de l'Ecole du Dimanche de Sion, 1926', *Sion Chapel Sunday School Minute Book, 1891-1937,* J/C/AK/A/5, Methodist Collection, Jersey Archive.

114   Minute of the meeting held on January 5th 1923, *Georgetown Chapel Sunday School Minute Book, 1919-36, op. cit.*; Minute of the meeting held on March 12th 1903, Grove Place Chapel Trust Minute Book, 1845-1924, *op. cit.*

115   Constitution of Society of Christian Endeavour for Bible Christian Youth, Undated, in *Young People's Society of Christian Endeavour Minute Book, 1893-1912,* J/C/J/A/1, Methodist Collection, Jersey Archive.

116   Carter, *op. cit.,* p.30; Minute of the meeting held on February 27th 1892, *French Circuit Sunday School Council Minutes, 1892-1922,* J/C/D/A/4, Methodist Collection, Jersey Archive; Georgetown Chapel Sunday School, Minute of the meeting held November 28th 1919, *Georgetown Chapel Sunday School Minute Book, 1919-36,* op. cit.; see also Bailey *et al.,* Disciplining youthful Methodist bodies, *op. cit.*

117   Anonymous, *Newscutting relating to the centenary celebrations of Les Frères Chapel Sunday school,* 1932, J/C/Z/G/2 Methodist Collection, Jersey Archive

118   Bailey *et al., op. cit.*

119   After Bourdieu, *op. cit.,* p.49 (citing G. Davy, *Eléments de sociologie,* Paris, Vrin, 1950, p.233).

120   Minutes of the meetings held on March 14th and September 12th 1925, *French Circuit Sunday School Council Minute Book, 1922-1941,* J/C/D/A/4, Methodist Collection, Jersey Archive.

121 *Ibid.*

122 Moore, op. cit., p. 112-14; Anonymous, *Bicentenary of Methodism in Jersey*, op. cit.; D. M. Chapman, *Chapel and Swastika: Methodism in the Channel Islands during the German Occupation 1940-1945*, Jersey, ELSP, 2009, pp.57-62.

123 Moore, *op. cit.*, pp.112-13.

124 Spence, *A brief history of Jèrriais, op. cit.*, p.2.

125 Bourdieu, *op. cit.*, p.234-35; pp.167-68.

126 Attachment to one's own chapel also being felt in the island's other circuits.

127 Moore, *op. cit.*, p.125-27; T. Nicholas, *An occasional paper written at the time of the Jersey celebrations to mark liberation from German occupation 60 years ago and the Methodists intention to implement change in response to their internal study document entitled "Shaped for Mission"*, Unpublished paper, Société Jersiaise, 2005, p.3.

128 I am grateful to Dr. John Le Gresley and Mrs. Jean Treleven for their discussion of these points.

129 'Photocopy of a document declaring in full the terms of the Model Trust Deed of the Methodist Church formed in 1932 by the union of the Wesleyan Methodist, Primitive Methodist and United Methodist Churches and recognising the validity in Jersey of the Model Deed.', 1933, J/C/B/D/A/3, Methodist Collection, Jersey Archive.

130 'Photocopy of a document', *op. cit.*

131 'Methodist Union Celebrations: Sunday October 2, 1932', *French Circuit Sunday School Council Minute Book, 1922-1941*, J/C/D/A/6, Methodist Collection, Jersey Archive.

132 Anonymous, United Methodism: Great day of witness – imposing procession of scholars, *The [Jersey] Evening Post*, Monday October 3rd 1932.

133 Anonymous, United Methodism: Great day of witness, *op. cit.*

134 *Ibid.*

135 *Ibid.*

136 Harvey *et al.*, Parading the Cornish subject, *op. cit.*

137 Bourdieu, *op. cit.*, pp.185-86; pp.234-35.

138 Spence, *A brief history of Jèrriais, op. cit.*, pp.3-4; Hublart, *op. cit.*, p.23.

139 Cracknell and White, *op. cit.*, pp.209-42.

140 'Règles de l'association', *Les Frères Chapel Christian Association Minute Book, 1907-1921*, J/C/Z/A/1, Methodist Collection, Jersey Archive; cf. *Young People's Society of Christian Endeavour Minute Book, 1893-1912*, J/C/J/A/1, Methodist Collection, Jersey Archive.

141 Minutes of meetings held on May 2nd 1936, February 7th 1939 and October 23rd 1939, *Jersey Council of Young Methodism Minute Book, 1935-1946*, J/C/AY/A/1, Methodist

Collection, Jersey Archive; Membership card of Young Methodism at Les Augrès Chapel, 1935-1936, J/C/Y/D/2, Methodist Collection, Jersey Archive.

142   Minute of the meeting held on November 30th 1926, *Bethlehem Chapel Wesley Guild Minute Book, 1926-1954*, J/C/L/A/4, Methodist Collection, Jersey Archive.

143   Minute of the meeting held on December 15th 1931, *Carmel Chapel Leaders Minute Book, 1919-1968*, J/C/M/A/4, Methodist Collection, Jersey Archive; Minute of the meeting held on January 17th 1930, *Grove Place Chapel Wesley Guild Executive Meeting Minute Book, 1913-1939*, J/C/W/A/2, Methodist Collection, Jersey Archive; Minute of the meeting held on January 29th 1920, *Grove Place Chapel Trust Minute Book, 1845-1924, op. cit.*

144   Minute of the meeting held on October 29th 1932, *Grove Place Chapel Trust Minute Book, 1825-1954*, J/C/W/A/3, Methodist Collection, Jersey Archive; Minutes of the meetings held on January 17th 1930 and October 15th 1935, Grove Place Chapel Wesley Guild Executive Meeting Minute Book, 1913-1939, *op. cit.*; Membership card of Young Methodism at Les Augrès Chapel, *op. cit.*

145   Minute of the meeting held on January 27th 1922, *Grove Place Chapel Trust Minute Book, 1845-1924, op. cit.*; Letter from Rev. G. Allen to D. C. Le Seeleur dated 1928 in *St Martins Chapel Wesley Guild Committee Minute Book, 1922-1990*, J/C/AE/A/2, Methodist Collection, Jersey Archive.

146   M. Monteil, *L'Emigration française vers Jersey 1850-1950*, Aix-en-Provence, Publications de l'Université de Provence, 2005 (see also the recent English translation published by the Société Jersiaise, entitled *French emigration to Jersey, 1850-1950*); Kelleher, *op. cit.*, pp.258-59.

147   Monteil, *L'Emigration française vers Jersey, op. cit.*, pp.126-32 ; D. Moore, *Deo Gratias: A history of the French Catholic Church in Jersey 1790-2007*, Jersey, Les Amitiés Franco-Britanniques de Jersey/Maison de la Normandie et de la Manche/Seaflower Books, 2007.

148   Kelleher, *op. cit.*, pp.258-59.

149   Moore, *Deo Gratias, op. cit.*, p.137.

150   Moore, *op. cit.*; Monteil, *op. cit.*; See also: Minute of the meeting held on June 19th 1950, *Ministers Fraternal Minute Book*, Methodist Collection, Jersey Archive.

151   Monteil, *op. cit.*, pp.249-52;

152   F. Le Maistre, *The Jersey language in its present state: the passing of a Norman heritage*, London, Jersey Society in London, 1947, pp.4-8; Spence, *A brief history of Jèrriais, op. cit.*, pp.6-9; Kelleher, *op. cit.*, p.134; Monteil, *op. cit.*, pp.249-52.

153   See: M. Jones, *Jersey Norman French: A linguistic study of an obsolescent dialect*, Oxford, Blackwell, 2001; G. Price, French in the Channel Islands, *op. cit.* N. B. The States of Jersey passed a law permitting English to be used in their debates in 1900.

154 *Plan of Services held in the French Circuit*, 1939, J/C/D/E/43, Methodist Collection, Jersey Archive.

155 Le Maistre, *The Jersey language in its present state*, *op. cit.*, p.9; Spence, Le sort de la francophonie à Jersey, *op. cit.*, pp.171-72.

156 See: N. Le Ruez, *Jersey Occupation Diary: her story of the German Occupation,1940-1945*, Jersey, Seaflower Books, 2003; P. Sanders, *The British Channel Islands under German Occupation 1940-1945*, Jersey, Jersey Heritage Trust; D. M. Chapman, *Chapel and swastika*, *op. cit.*

157 See, for example: Minute of the meeting held on September 5th 1940, *Grove Place Circuit Local Preachers Minute Book, 1910-1946*, J/C/D/A/5, Methodist Collection, Jersey Archive; *Georgetown Chapel Cradle Roll Register, 1936-1972*, J/C/T/B/1, Methodist Collection, Jersey Archive. On evacuation numbers, see M. Ginns, *Jersey Occupied: The German armed forces in Jersey, 1940-45*, Jersey, Channel Island Publishing, 2009, p.16.

158 See, for example: Nicholas, *An occasional paper*, *op. cit.*, pp.1-2.

159 Minute of the meeting held on May 7th 1946, *Bethlehem Chapel Wesley Guild Minute Book, 1926-1954*, J/C/L/A/4, Methodist Collection, Jersey Archive; Minute of the meeting held on August 21st 1940, *Georgetown Chapel Leaders Meeting Minute Book, 1938-1964*, J/C/T/A/4, Methodist Collection, Jersey Archive; Minutes of the meetings held on Jun 11th 1940 and February 10th 1941, *Minutes for the Women's Work Council of the Channel Islands District, 1932-1955*, J/C/A/A/4(A), Methodist Collection, Jersey Archive; cf. Anonymous, *Official Report of the English Circuit for the period of the German occupation of Jersey, 1940-1945*, J/C/E/H/6, Methodist Collection, Jersey Archive.

160 *List of the Annual Exchange by the Jersey Free Church Council of Ministers between Chapels, 1940-1946*, J/C/AS/F/2, Methodist Collection, Jersey Archive; Minute of the meeting held on June 20th 1944, *Minute Book for the Sunday School Council at Carmel Chapel, 1886-1963*, J/C/M/A/3, Methodist Collection, Jersey Archive.

161 Minute of the meeting held on May 26th 1943, *Sion Chapel Leaders Meeting Minute Book, 1904-1961*, J/C/AK/A/7, Methodist Collection, Jersey Archive.

162 Minute of the meeting held on February 10th 1941, *Minutes for the Women's Work Council of the Channel Islands District, 1932-1955*, *op. cit.*

163 Minute of the meeting held on August 26th 1941, *Minutes for the Women's Work Council of the Channel Islands District, 1932-1955*, *op. cit.*

164 Minute of the meeting held on June 14th 1945, *Grove Place Circuit Quarterly Meeting Minute Book, 1941-1964*, J/C/D/A/7, Methodist Collection, Jersey Archive.

165 Moore, *Methodism in the Channel Islands*, *op. cit.*, p.157.

166 Spence, *A brief history of Jèrriais*, *op. cit.* See also D. Edbrooke, Champion of the Island's unique selling point – its native language, *Jersey Evening Post*, 10 November 2018, p.26-27.

167 Jones, *Jersey Norman French, op. cit.*; Spence, *A brief history of Jèrriais, op. cit.*; Spence, Le sort de la francophonie à Jersey, *op. cit.*

168 Minute of the meeting held on December 12th 1918, *English Circuit Quarterly Meeting Minute Book, 1888-1908*, J/C/E/A/2, Methodist Collection, Jersey Archive; Minute of the meeting held on January 19th 1923, *Grove Place Chapel Trust Minute Book, 1845-1924*, op. cit.

169 Minute of the meeting held on March 15th 1934, *Jersey Wesley Circuit Quarterly Meeting Minute Book, 1921-1944*, J/C/E/A/4, Methodist Collection, Jersey Archive.

170 Minute of the meeting held on December 9th 1937, Jersey Wesley Circuit Quarterly Meeting Minute Book, 1921-1944, *op. cit.*

171 Minute of the meeting held on October 29th 1945, *Jersey Island Committee Minute Book, 1945-1947*, J/C/AT/1, Methodist Collection, Jersey Archive.

172 Anonymous letter sent to Rev. Colin Roberts, Undated, in Document 6, Methodist Box File, Lord Coutanche Library, Société Jersiaise.

173   Rev. Rider was Superintendent of the Grove Place and later Wesley Grove circuit.

174 '*Scheme for Amalgamation of Methodist Churches in Jersey into One Circuit, as agreed by Committee, 3 April 1946*', Document 6, Methodist Box File, Lord Coutanche Library, Société Jersiaise.

175 Letter from the Methodist War Emergency Fund to the Jersey Island [Amalgamation] Committee, dated May 7th 1946, in *Jersey Island Committee Minute Book, 1945-1947, op. cit.*

176 'Report of the Meeting of the Conference Commission and the Jersey Amalgamation Committee', April 25th 1946, in *Jersey Island Committee Minute Book, 1945-1947, op. cit.*; Letter from Rev. W. C. Fell to the Amalgamation Committee of the Jersey Circuits, dated September 27th 1946, in *Jersey Island Committee Minute Book, 1945-1947*, op. cit.; Minute of Special Church Meeting held at Les Landes Chapel, May 23rd 1946, Document 6, Methodist Box File, Lord Coutanche Library, Société Jersiaise.

177 Minute of the meeting held on November 29th 1946, *Jersey Island Committee Minute Book, 1945-1947, op. cit.*

178 Anonymous, 'Wesleyans Will Be "One" Again: Island's Two Churches To Unite', *Jersey Morning News*, August 27th, 1947, in Scrapbook containing newscuttings relating to Methodist news, activities, members and Chapels, 1945-1959, J/C/BQ/2, Methodist Collection, Jersey Archive.

179 *Plan of services for Wesley Grove Circuit*, 1947, J/C/F/B/1, Methodist Collection, Jersey Archive.

180 *Grove Place Chapel Centenary Souvenir Booklet*, 1947, J/C/W/G/1, Methodist Collection, Jersey Archive.

181 *Report on the proposed union of the English Circuit and French Circuit*, 1947, J/C/E/H/7, Methodist Collection, Jersey Archive; Anonymous, 'Wesleyans Will Be "One" Again: Island's Two Churches To Unite', *Jersey Morning News, op. cit.*

182 *Grove Place Chapel Centenary Souvenir Booklet, op. cit.*

183 See, for example: *Order of service at Ebenezer Chapel for the Bicentenary of Methodism in Jersey celebrations*, [1974], J/C/N/E/1, Methodist Collection, Jersey Archive.

184 Hublart, *Le français de Jersey, op. cit.*, see Note 46.

Select Bibliography

The following works provide further insight on the history of Methodism in Jersey.

Anonymous, *Bicentenary of Methodism in Jersey, Channel Islands 1774-1974* (Jersey: JEP Publications, 1974).

Arnett, H., *Handbook of Methodist history in Jersey* (Jersey: Jersey Evening Post, 1909).

Brée, P. E., *The origin and development of Methodism in La Rocque* (Published privately: booklet available from the Jersey Archive, reference J/C/X/F/2, 1932).

Broughton, K. F., *Methodism and an island community: Jersey 1770-1870* (Open University: Unpublished thesis, 1995).

Carter, D., *A Jersey childhood* (Jersey: CTV Publications, 1989).

Chapman, D. M., *Chapel and Swastika: Methodism in the Channel Islands during the German Occupation 1940-1945* (Jersey: ELSP, 2009).

Guiton, F., *Histoire du Méthodisme Wesleyen dans les Iles de la Manche* (London: John Mason, 1846).

Hill, R., *Circuits of capital: placing the end of francophone Methodism in Jersey, 1900-1950* (University of Exeter: Unpublished B.Sc. thesis, 2010).

Hublart, C., 1979. Le Français de Jersey. Unp. thesis, Université L'État à Mons

Jersey Methodist Church Study Group, *The Methodist Church in Jersey: The way forward* (Published privately: book available from the Jersey Library, shelf mark J287, 1986).

Kelleher, J. D., *The triumph of the country: rural community in nineteenth-century Jersey* (Dublin: John Appleby Publishing, 1994).

Langlois, S. M. A., *An investigation of the language issue in the Channel Islands, based upon a case study of Methodism in Jersey* (Herts College of Further Education: Unpublished B.Ed. thesis, 1978).

Le Boutillier, F., *First Tower Methodist Church 1847-1997* (Published privately: booklet available from the Jersey Library, shelf mark J287, 1997)

Le Cornu, J., *One hundred not out! The story of a Mission* (Jersey: Samarès Methodist Church/Seaflower Books, 2003).

Le Lievre, M., *Histoire du Méthodisme dans les Iles de la Manche 1784-1884* (Paris: Librairie Evangélique, 1885).

Le Ruez, N., *Jersey Occupation Diary: her story of the German Occupation, 1940-1945* (Jersey: Seaflower Books, 2003).

Marett, D., *Chapelle Wesleyenne 1851-2001: Celebrating the one hundred and fiftieth anniversary of St Martin's Methodist Chapel* (Jersey: Les Rues, 2000).

Moore, R. D., *Methodism in the Channel Islands* (London: Epworth Press, 1952).

Morley, G. R., *The story of Methodism at St. Aubin, Jersey* (Jersey: Trustees of St Aubin Methodist Church/Bennett Brothers, 1967).

Mourant, L., *History of Eden Chapel* (Published privately: booklet available from the Jersey Archive, reference J/C/P/E/1, 1983).

Nicholas, Rev. T., *The Bible Christians in Jersey* (Jersey: Published privately, book available from the Jersey Library, shelf mark J287, 2002).

Nicholas, Rev. T., *The story of Methodism in Gorey* (Jersey: Published privately, booklet available from the Jersey Library, shelf mark J287, 2005).

Index